THE BLACK HOURS

MODERN DEMONIC EXPERIENCES & FOLKLORE

VICTORIA JAYE

AN AMERICAN HAUNTINGS INK BOOK

Dedication
To my mom, who believed me first and encouraged all my weird interests.

THE BLACK HOURS

MODERN DEMONIC EXPERIENCES & FOLKLORE

© COPYRIGHT 2025 BY VICTORIA JAYE

Published by American Hauntings Ink
301 East Broadway - Alton IL - 62002
www.americanhauntingsink.com

Cover Design by April Slaughter
Interior Design by Troy Taylor

Printed in the United States of America

INTRODUCTION

This book is titled *The Black Hours* because I'm trying to capture the feelings associated with a demonic presence. When a person is around this kind of intense evil and malice directed at oneself or their loved ones, it can feel like the complete absence of light and that it will never get better. My working definition of a demon is a spirit in that they exist without bodies, possess abilities greater than that of humans, rendering them inhuman; they are hyper intelligent and react negatively to Christian iconography[1]. Demons are often described as blacker-than-night or blacker-than-black when one manifests[2]. I prefer to identify them by what they can do, not what they are since nobody truly knows for sure - -religion offers an explanation but not facts. It all comes down to what you believe. In the research of this book, I have examined multiple perspectives including that of demonolaters, or those who worship demons, to better understand demonic behavior. I consistently challenge my own beliefs due to added information being uncovered—I may get things wrong in this pursuit. My only hope is that my research helps people as it was intended to and that my classification efforts hold up when identifying the behaviors of demons.

CLASSIFICATION ERRORS

There's been an inherent classification error regarding demons and jinn that has existed for an awfully long time; Islam conflates the two at times[3]. In Judaism at one point in time, everything that wasn't of God—jinn, once-worshipped deities, other types of entities—were overarchingly labeled a demon[4]. This is not a criticism of Islam or Judaism for their beliefs, everyone reserves the right to believe how they want in their religion. However, whilst examining famous demonic cases such as Annaliese Michel's, I found that jinn possession can be accidentally mistaken for demonic. In the Michel case, the entity possessing her often wouldn't come out when bade to by invoking God or Jesus. That piece of phenomena, beside the fact that it simply wasn't intense enough to be a demon made me reevaluate the case entirely. A demon will react in the strongest possible terms to Christian iconography, texts, and will bend to the authority of God. The fact that it didn't means that it had the free will to resist; jinn do have free will, according to their lore[5]. Culture always works best in its context, so a Quran might have benefitted Michel more during her exorcism, but if one didn't know about jinn, then Christian religious texts would be the obvious choice to expel a demon.

Jinn behaviors, it must be said, are not always as malevolent towards humans[6], but they can be since Michel tragically died along with others dealing with malevolent jinn. Jinn and demons have similarities, but are not the same entity and over time, they have been mistaken as such. This is an easy mistake with translation and the concept of invisibility in Islam being under the general term "jinn" umbrella[7]. If the very molecules in your body are not telling you to run, to get away from this horrific entity as fast as you can, then it is not a demon based on the narratives that currently exist[8]. Every single narrative about demons tells about a moment of being in the presence of pure evil, of extreme malice, and the desire to leave immediately when sensing them in the vicinity[9].

WITCHES' USE OF THE WORD "DEMON"

I have a profound respect for the witch and Pagan communities; I've found them to be loving, caring people who will help one out with spiritual problems in a second—and who have helped me personally with spirits that were pestering me. If that offends you, this may not be the book for you; I know how Christianity feels about witchcraft, but I do not share that opinion.

When witches today usually refer to a spirit as a "demon" they are mostly referring to the Ancient Greek *daemon* definition of a demon, meaning a spirit of great power[10]. They don't mean Christianized meanings of the word; demons, then, are thought to be more like intermediaries or land spirits of great power that can divine the future[11]. I do caution the use of the word in that context, only because it cannot be separated from the Christian or horror movie definition in public discourse. For that reason, it's unwise to continue to use it knowing most people don't understand the difference. An example of this is from a discussion I had with Vanessa Walilko on her podcast, *Personal Pans*, when it comes to the common usage of the word, "demon". An example that came up from Vanessa was people trying to reclaim the swastika from Nazis; yes, at one point in time, this maligned symbol meant something else but we're not in that point of time. If you advertise you worship demons when you mean daemons, the public will not understand your meaning. If you mean a demon in the sense of Christianity or horror context, and I say this with the utmost respect, I don't think that's what you're worshipping—at least not from the definition I'm studying. When I say demon, I am isolating a specific type of spirit that announces itself with a feeling of horrific evil, terrible sounds, disgusting smells, and eventually causes harm to humans just by being around them[12]. They <u>never</u> help people; demonic behavior suggests only hatred for humans, so daimons could be jinn or a shedim—a subsect of Jewish jinn that became the overarching word for demons[13]. The knowledge and help bestowed by "demons" and even sexual experiences people have claimed to have had sound exactly like pre-Islamic beliefs about jinn[14], which might be what people think are demons or daemons[15]. Enochian Watchers—who were figures sent by God to watch over humanity but mated with human women instead also appear to have similar qualities as daemons[16].

I genuinely want to know what is believed about demons in every country by each group of people—but that's a bigger endeavor that this book cannot cover. For this project, I'm acknowledging that witches have a unique perspective on the

7

subject that deserves further inquiry, but that it may not be the entity I'm studying. *The Black Hours* is my understanding currently, and I accept there are times that I could be wrong, especially if my research is fundamentally flawed in any way. It is not my intention to send out misinformation in a world that's already riddled with it.

PARANORMAL TELEVISION

The main contributor to misinformation is paranormal TV[17]. As far as I know, no studies have been formally conducted on the misinformation presented, but it is a well-known fact in the paranormal research and investigating communities that nothing you see on TV is real. Demons aren't common; they're incredibly rare, even in the world of paranormal investigators, as I have often been told. People emailed me what they thought were demonic experiences after my thesis was published online, and I can confidently say that only one of them sounded even remotely demonic out of hundreds. This was because there was a distinctly evil presence with multiple phenomena that heralded its identity: horrific stenches, a witnessed black figure, and vanishing acts among other things.

This statement is not meant to ridicule anyone who reached out; it was very brave to send something so personal and scary to a stranger. I'm merely pointing out that paranormal TV has gotten pervasive to the point that every negative supernatural experience is assumed to be demon. This is false. True demonic experiences are so rare that investigators should never assume something is a demon initially, but Christianity, horror, and paranormal TV have pushed a false narrative that they're everywhere.

There are people working in the paranormal who don't believe in demons at all, which is understandable if you've never come across one in the entire time you've investigated; I've been told this and have seen it expressed on Twitter many times by paranormal investigators. Paranormal TV will call anything demonic to boost views because it's much higher stakes than other types of spirits. Demon as a descriptor implies serious bodily danger and heightened supernatural activity, which is an entertainment goldmine. I view paranormal TV as being merely entertainment, but the problem is that a sizable portion of people watching these TV shows view it as gospel and 100% real—this even happens with horror movies. Experts brought in are even told to lie and say it's a demon when it isn't, which I've heard about from those who refused. The world of entertainment is not absolute fact and most paranormal researchers are trying to debunk what paranormal TV has exaggerated. Be careful what you believe and remember that while real things can happen on camera, most of it is entertainment intended to make the network and stars of the show more money.

CHRISTIAN FEAR

Christianity in recent years has been pushing the narrative that we should be more afraid of demons. A perfect example of this was in July 2022 when there had been multiple mass shootings. It was implied by Christian, conservative media that at least one of them was the work of a demon because there were pentagrams and a "Satanic manifesto"[18]. Demons are so rare that nobody should be afraid of them to the level that is being pushed by Christian propaganda. To me, there was nothing demonic about that boy or his manifesto; it looked like religious trauma paired with incel-driven mental illness. Demons can influence mental health and make conditions worse that previously existed, but demons themselves aren't the root cause of mental illness—selling that narrative is dangerous. Mental illness is real and should be taken care of first if you believe a demon has infested your life; an exorcist will never be able to solve a mental health problem.

It is irresponsible at best to claim demons are making people shoot other people when mental health exists and is often overlooked. At worst, you're scaring people[19]. Demons don't make humans pull the trigger; remember that we have free will and agency, something we're told in the Bible, too. Demons can be involved in tragedies, I will admit that, but this is a rare occurrence. I believe from all my research that people have a choice to hurt others in the event of demonic infestation. Possession, something deeply feared by Christians, is a process–demons cannot just get inside you, or we'd all have demons in or around us currently. According to Christianity, everyone sins. Yes, a demon can eventually possess someone, but they often hop out of the body because their presence makes the body break down and the person regains their will momentarily then the oppression process has to start again[20]. Just because something is possible doesn't make it probable–spreading fear and misinformation is not helping anyone. There needs to be a process of elimination in determining the type of spirit in residence without jumping to conclusions.

THE WARRENS

There's also the question of whether to use Ed and Lorraine Warrens' work. There are rumors that Ed had an ongoing relationship with a minor and that their books were heavily exaggerated to make more money[21]. Ed and Lorraine Warren brought the paranormal into the limelight with cases such as the Annabelle doll, the Amityville Horror infestation, and the Perron family case of The Conjuring fame. They also spread, perhaps unwittingly, Satanic Panic and fear about demons, which aren't common enough to be afraid of in the first place. I'm using their books because they are contributing to demonic folklore, exaggerated or not, and I don't feel I can fully discuss demonic folklore without using their work. In the future with more demonic experiences becoming known, this may someday be possible. In my area of study of folklore studies, it doesn't matter whether it's true but whether people believe it's true. I hesitate to call anything they claimed fact because of what is alleged about them. I used their work for my thesis and this book, but I have a healthy amount of skepticism about believing their versions of events. On the other hand, I think the phenomena they've mentioned is something they've personally witnessed or have heard about. The phenomena they talk about in their rumored exaggerations have come up in other narratives, exactly as the Warrens described in cases that are not connected to them. It could be that they're influencing the overall process of demonic folklore where all stories are built entirely off the ones they told first. Yet, most cases of demonic infestation have people who didn't know about Ed and Lorraine Warren, their work, and didn't even think it was a demon once they realized it was supernatural. To the people it's happening to, they think they're the only ones and are unaware that other people do go through the same thing. I defend my use of the Warrens' work for that reason; besides that, this book is based in folklore, and there is value in the examples given of how the phenomena manifests. I'm not endorsing them since I understand the irritation and outright hatred the paranormal community has for them since it directly contributed to the demon narrative going on now. Just know that I'm not using their work thinking it's gospel. It's not; the Warrens were people, and nobody's perfect. This is not a book glorifying them or their work. I mined their books for demonic folklore. I didn't know them personally, so I can't comment on the kind of people they were or weren't.

What I do know is that they were the first to bring demonology into the public sphere; Ed and Lorraine Warren were educators and demonologists. Ed worked with the Catholic Church on exorcisms and Lorraine was a medium who often assisted with cases by using her psychic abilities. Being the first makes you automatically problematic since your work will be critiqued for decades to come with everything you unknowingly did wrong. I'm the first folklorist to specialize in the demonic as my subject area; I'm hoping my work will stand up better to time, but I'm bound to get something wrong somewhere that only the future will be able to realize. For now, I'm doing the best I can with the tools I currently have.

PSYCHIC ABILITY AND MY FAITH

I am psychic in that I have psychic abilities, but it's unlike what is shown on television talking to the dead or seeing spirits. I don't need you to believe me, and it's okay if you don't. I am currently clairaudient (clear hearing), claircognizant (clear knowing), clairsentient (clear feeling), geomantic (I feel the energy of cities/areas), a tiny bit of mediumship (sometimes spirits try to talk to me), and a small amount of psychometry (I can sometimes pull information from photographs). Mediums became extremely popular during the movement of Spiritualism in the nineteenth century; people clamored to see the spectacle of life after death[22]. My abilities are not as marketable, nor did I know much about it until I was an adult and exploring spirituality for myself.

I've experienced this my entire life, starting with prophetic dreams at age three and clairaudience chiming in when I was about eight or nine. Everyone in my family is psychically gifted, though it manifests in diverse ways. I love being the way that I am, though it isn't always fun or easy to be psychic. It can be a burden. I don't go into demonically infested places and help people directly for this reason. It's not because I'm afraid. I know that demons prey on psychic ability and can use it against someone. Why would I give something that so clearly hates humans that advantage over me? If my abilities were compromised, I wouldn't be able to help, so unfortunately, I must leave the work of going in to help families to demonologists—something I don't consider myself to be since by definition, I don't do what demonologists do in action or research.

It's important that I discuss my faith because inevitably in this sort of work, it'll come up. People want to know where I'm coming from on this subject. I believe in God. I don't feel comfortable calling myself a Christian when I don't believe many things Christians do. There's a lot of Christian-led hatred for people who are different because they don't believe the same as you do, and how it seems like many Christians cherry-pick the parts of the Bible they want to support while ignoring the others. This work and folklore in general have made it clear to me that other types of spirits exist and that it's not all angels or demons. I believe in God yes, but I believe in other things, too. Witches, Pagans, and Satanists are some of the best people you'll ever meet while I've watched Christians pass judgment on others for having paranormal activity in their lives and not offering to help. When I had spiritual psychic problems, a Pagan friend and another friend on the left-handed magic path offered to help and did. I needed help improving my psychic protections because I was being bothered constantly by spirits, and they showed me how. I won't listen to slander about other groups of people because you fear them or their magic. The history of Christianity itself is bloody, and I won't stand for hatred on my social media or anywhere else where I have a say.

Not every Christian is hateful, so if none of this sounds like you, then great, you're one of the people actually upholding Jesus' teachings. My entire purpose is to help others, but that doesn't mean I believe what you believe. I believe what the research tells me: my research, and other people's. If you want to argue doctrine, argue it with someone else – I'm a folklorist, not a theologist. I try to keep my belief system out of it to keep things scientific but yes, I've read the Bible many times and done the necessary research.

HOW DEMONS ENTER PEOPLE'S LIVES

There are perceivable patterns from occultism and demonology explaining how the process of demonic infestation happens. Demons can't just come into people's lives; if they could enter simply because they wanted to, demons would be more common in our world. The first way that these entities can enter one's life is through the Law of Invitation, or by opening a door, often thought to be through black magic or incorrectly thought to be through Ouija boards–if one doesn't know how to use the board or close the session, then there is the possibility of a dangerous entity messing with people's lives[23]. Another way is through the corruption in a person's soul that leads to evil actions, called the Law of Attraction[24]. This is when you do something so sick and twisted that demons become attracted to your soul; in effect, they want to hang out with you because you're such a terrible part of humanity.

What I call the Unwarranted Entry idea of why demons manifest is also a possibility but is extremely rare: it is when a person neither invited nor attracted a demon, but it enters a person's life anyway, which breaks the laws that are thought to bind them[25]. Another part of Unwarranted Entry is when a practitioner of dark magic, defined as magic intending to take or cause harm, sends a demon after a person because it is thought in the occult that these practitioners can control demons for their own purposes[26]. The last reason demons are thought to come into people's lives is through what I have deemed the Already Inhabited category, meaning that a demon was already in residence of a dwelling and people either moved in or crossed its path by accident, often without prior knowledge that anything was already living there[27]. The reason demons are such a horrifically negative presence to us, according to multiple religious interpretations, is because they wish humans harm and desire our torment[28]. The theory is that this malice can be sensed on an evolutionary level, when our bodies are in fight-or-flight mode due to our hormones responding to a dangerous situation towards something we fear; this is because it intends to cause us harm[29]. Other types of supernatural memorates, or firsthand experiences, have been described as frightening and negative but not necessarily evil. What seems to distinguish the demonic from other supernatural phenomena is that people sense that it is unholy evil and deeply malicious towards them. These people expressed trouble forgetting their terror. The only similar feeling of evil from a supernatural narrative that has come up is the terrifying panic of the Old Hag or Mara experience; I am not looking at narratives involving sleep for this reason[30]. All memorates included here are from times when people were awake.

The process of a demon coming into one's life comes in stages: encroachment, infestation, oppression, possession, and death. Encroachment is when a demon looks for a foothold in one's life; demons do not come through cracks in one's life (erroneously believed to be caused by sin) but fully formed doorways. Infestation is when a demon moves into a place and causes havoc—the phenomena begins small and progresses into terrifying manifestations of power. Oppression is when a person is singled out to break down their mind for possession, which is when the body and mind is taken over by the demon, which, if left untreated, results in the person's death[31].

Demons, according to the narratives, can appear how they want to—sometimes even as apparitions, which are recognizably human spirits. Demonic spirits are set apart from ghostly inhabitants by their non-human, often horrific appearances[32]. This is either because they cannot appear human completely or they do not wish to, though my educated guess is the former. If they do appear human, there is always a flawed appearance that is terrifying to behold like dark holes instead of eyes or decaying and corpse-like in presentation[33].

PREFACE

I specialize in demonic phenomena, narratives, and experiences, and I have my master's degree from Utah State University. I openly believe in the paranormal and especially demons, though there is a lot of incorrect Christian folklore surrounding this type of entity. Religion, in its way, is also a folklore source to understand mostly how ancient people understood demons and their own environments. If you've read my thesis *In the Presence of Evil: Demonic Perception Narratives* some of the same information is in here, but there are several parts being expanded that had previously been pared down or cut out entirely of the thesis. I'm trying to include as much phenomena as possible to expose that demons have observable patterns.

I had a terrifying experience with possession when I was nineteen years old, in 2014. My thesis research yielded that it was not a demonic presence as I'd previously thought, and unfortunately, I unwittingly provided misinformation in my thesis when I said it was a demon. Not knowing better, I truly believed that, but my research has proved me wrong. I believe currently that it was either a dybbuk, a jinn intrusion, or something similar. Dybbukim (the plural form of dybbuk) are from Jewish folklore and are the spirits of people who have died that are barred from Heaven and Hell, so they are forced to wander the earth[34]. Jinn are made from "smokeless fire", created by Allah before humans, and from my research, they exist somewhere between humans and demons in behavior since they display traits of both. In Islam, demons and jinn are often believed to be one in the same, but it is only certain types of jinn that are specifically evil[35]. All jinn can possess people, but only evil ones break that sacred boundary[36]. Like humans, jinn have free will; do not mistake them for genies because that isn't what they are.[37]Genies are a Western conceptualization of the jinn; they don't grant wishes nor can they truly be controlled[38]. More information will be provided on jinn in Chapter Two.

HOW TO USE THIS BOOK

This book covers only more modern cases of demonic encroachment, infestation, oppression, and possession since demons in antiquity and medieval times have already been studied extensively in academia. The way this book is formatted is with the beginning chapters designed to ground one in the subject of demons and how they're viewed by the three Abrahamic religions (Christianity, Islam, and Judaism), other frequent questions answered, and then the classification system itself. Next to each piece of phenomena is a check box; if you believe there is a demonic presence in your life or in another person's life that you know, check off any phenomena that you know has happened. I'm formatting it this way in the hope that it can be useful to paranormal investigators as well as anyone who suspects something paranormal is going on in their lives.

Each section of the book is divided into the different senses a demon activates: sight, sound, smell, and feeling. This book is meant to be written on; use the check boxes literally if you think a demon is interfering with your life. The more checkboxes you have, the more likely you are to have a demonic presence but be aware that some phenomena shows up in other narratives unrelated to demons such as footsteps, cold spots, or voices speaking aloud. The difference between a demon and another entity is that feeling that you are in the presence of evil that means you harm, the intensity level, and malice. Any other type of haunting will not be even close to the malicious harm of a demon, which the experiences directly underneath the phenomena will illustrate.

A last critical point; people often only believe something supernatural is happening when they witness it. Seeing, for the skeptic, is believing. They could feel all sorts of things, hear strange things all the time and even smell horrific things but it is only when a supernatural presence is witnessed that people realize it isn't all in their head. There is a great capacity for ignoring what is being sensed because it doesn't fit rational explanations. Trust yourself and trust that your body can sense something is wrong even if you're not focusing on it.

[1] Victoria Jaye, 2021."In the Presence of Evil: Demonic Perception Narratives", Thesis.
[2] Ibid.
[3] Ibid.
[4] Muhammad Vandestra, *The World of Angels (Malaikah) and Jinn (Demons) in Islam Religion.* 2021: 7; Amira El-Zein, *Islam, Arabs, and the Intelligent World of the Jinn.* 2017: xi.
[5] John H. Walton and J. Harvey Walton, *Demons and Spirits in Biblical Theology: Reading the Biblical Text in Its Cultural and Literary Context.* 2019: 164, 239.
[6] Robert Lebling, *Legends of the Fire Spirits: Jinn and Genies from Arabia to Zanzibar.* 2011: 2.
[7] Amira El-Zein, "Islam, Arabs, and the Intelligent World of the Jinn", 2017: 18/52.
[8] Ibid. 34/39.
[9] Jaye, "In the Presence of Evil", 2021.
[10] Ibid
[11] El-Zein, 2017: xiv.
[12] Ibid, 57
[13] Jaye, "In the Presence of Evil," 2021.
[14] Annette Yoshiko Reed, Demons, Angels, and Writing in Ancient Judaism. 2020: 50; Lebling, 2011: 265.

[15] El-Zein, 2017: 28.

[16] Ibid. 50.

[17] The Book of Enoch: 7-8.

[18] Scott Craven," Why those TV ghost-hunting shows are transparently fake." 2017. https://www.azcentral.com/story/travel/arizona/2017/10/02/ghost-hunting-shows-fake/705566001/.

[19] Fox News Staff, "Parkland Shooter Nikolas Cruz's disturbing jailhouse drawings show images of mass murder, Satanic messages", 2022. https://www.fox13news.com/news/parkland-shooter-nikolas-cruzs-disturbing-jailhouse-drawings-show-images-of-mass-murder-satanic-messages.

[20] Alex Matsuo, Tiktok, "The Result of Saying Everything is a Demon." 2023.

[21] Caitlin Busch, "The Alleged True Story Behind the Real 'Conjuring' Couple is Vile", 2017. https://www.inverse.com/article/39376-conjuring-true-story-ed-lorraine-warren-alleged-underage-sex.

[22] Benjamin T. Guerrentz. "Spiritualism - Timeline Movement." https://www.thearda.com/us-religion/history/timelines/entry?etype=3&eid=67.

[23] Marie D. Jones and Larry Flaxman, "Demons, The Devil, and Fallen Angels", 2017: Loc 3071.

[24] Ibid. Loc 3074.

[25] Jaye, "In the Presence of Evil", 2021.

[26] Ibid.

[27] Jones and Flaxman, 2017: Loc 4314.

[28] Jaye, "In the Presence of Evil", 2021.

[29] Russell, Jeffrey Burton. The Prince of Darkness: Radical Evil and the Power of Good in History. 1989: 37.

[30] Harvard Health Publishing: Harvard Medical School; "Understanding the stress response", 2020.

[31] Jaye, "In the Presence of Evil", 2021.
David J. Hufford, The Terror that Comes in the Night: An Experience-Centered Study of Supernatural Assault Traditions. 1989: 27.

[32] Gerald Brittle, The Demonologist: The Extraordinary Career of Ed and Lorraine Warren. reprint 2013: 27

[33] Ibid. 18.

[34] Ibid. 18.

[35] Baal Kadmon, *Devils, Demons, and Ghosts in the Hebrew Tradition: Romancing the Sitra Achra.* 2019: 192.
[36] Lebling 2010: Loc 143; Vandestra 2019: 7.
[37] Lebling 2010: 2/64.
[38] Ibid. 2

MY EXPERIENCES

It may not be demonic, but I'm hoping my experience will open a dialogue with others who have had the same thing or something similar happen to them. All I truly know is that it had something to do with mirrors being pointed at my bed and my abilities as a psychic. Another person reached out with a similar experience who also had several mirrors pointed at her bed during these types of attacks. In early 2014, I was in a very dark headspace from multiple heartbreaks when it all started. First came the nightmares, of huge flesh-colored demons with gaping maws full of sharp teeth and soulless eyes, trying to chase me around the room. I was terrified of sleep because of what I knew I'd see, so I didn't sleep. I began throwing up food, unable to keep anything down. The lack of sleep produced terrifying hallucinations like that my father and my mother looked like other family members; I vividly saw different faces morph out of theirs. Then I had tactile hallucinations of being beaten and even the sexual assault of what felt like fingers entering me (another family member felt this at least once as well during this period). This is the hardest part to talk about. It felt so real, but it wasn't– I know that now.

My parents didn't understand why bruises bloomed on my face. They said it had to be makeup (it wasn't). That made no sense to me because I felt every hit. The bruises were real; they hurt when I touched them. Reality was bent, at least for me in my weakened state. Then I began to see things around the house: dark things. They hid in shadows, but I could see their eyes. Auditory hallucinations came next—some of the actor's lines changed as I watched a comfort movie, and they became more menacing in meaning. I knew something was coming, something very dark, and I couldn't stop it.

I was progressively getting worse, more delusional and my parents had to leave me alone one day. It wasn't their fault–they absolutely had to be somewhere else. I should not have left the house, but I feared it was coming for me. I was in pajamas and a robe; the neighbors called the cops on me. An ambulance eventually came and since this was in Las Vegas, everyone assumed I was on drugs. I had sores on my face from extreme stress causing cystic acne that wouldn't heal until I went home nor would anything else; bruises appeared up and down my arms randomly one day at home and didn't disappear the entire time I was in the hospital for two weeks.

They asked me stupid questions in the ambulance: Are you an alien? Are you Jesus? Are you possessed? That last one made me stop laughing at the ridiculousness of it all, had me consider. Was I possessed? I don't think I was just yet. Then I was talking about the darkness coming, swallowing me right before I was sedated, according to a nurse who talked to my mom. They administered three times the typical dose because my adrenaline was so high; I didn't want to sleep. I knew something bad would happen if I did.

When I awoke, something else was inside me. I woke up in the hospital, but something else was also looking out through my eyes, talking through me. I was there, but silent, unable to do anything except watch. My parents were there, and I spoke to them; told them something awful about me not being their child based on my blood type. (I know nothing about blood types.) This thing inside me felt smug and cruel but not truly evil. Then "I" didn't wake up for three days. Gone. I have absolutely no memory of the next few days until I awoke with a cigarette in my hand. I didn't smoke and still don't. I didn't even have my glasses–could this entity see without them? I'm near blind. It took a bit to figure out where my glasses were, where I was, and what had happened to me. Mental hospitals are confusing places; chaotic. I was scared and doped up with meds I didn't need that just made me sick and diagnosed with disorders I didn't have.

Having been misdiagnosed as bipolar schizophrenic, I was given medication that induced hallucinations, resulting in horrific headaches. My interactions with people were strange to say the least. The *confusion* was unrivaled; I couldn't make sense of anything happening, of why I couldn't go home. Here's the thing: I could have. I was told I could sign myself out when "I" wasn't there, so I was kept in this awful place. I felt evil everywhere in this mental institution, even to the point that I knew some of the other women wanted to hurt me. It had stirred them up. I was terrified and asked an orderly to sleep somewhere else. Thankfully, he somehow believed me, and I was shut in a room by myself until about four in the morning.

I don't know if it was my imagination, but it was like people were being used against me. They called me derogatory things as they passed by, then later apologized, said they don't know why they said it, and since the wing was open to men and women, I could feel a man with voices in his head being told to hurt me. This same random man in the ward asked all sorts of weird, inappropriate questions about marriage in the confines of where we were. It could be paranoia, I accept that, but that's not what I believe. I was in danger because whatever possessed me had been spat back out. It wanted back in, but I needed to black out again for that to happen. People said strange things, like, "Why are we all pretending we don't want her?" It felt like I was emitting some type of light, and they were coveting it, wanting it for themselves, crowding around to smother it until the light failed. I had one experience where I sat with a splitting headache on the ground, hurting and then a juice cart flipped over. They looked at me, astonished, but I was a good five feet away and still on the floor. My parents and my sister came to see me a few times, and that was always a tearful affair. I didn't want them to go. I feared being in that place, unprotected as I was.

A nurse took pity on me because I was so polite to her, calling my parents behind the hospital's back (they wanted to keep me in that godforsaken place for another six months). I had told her I thought I was pregnant. I wasn't. Not even possibly and I knew that, but the idea had been fed to me by another person in there with me. Like I was being told how to save myself because I was discharged the next day. My mom nearly cried when she saw me; I was too thin. My face hadn't healed, and the bruises were brighter somehow, like I was being fed from in that sick place. This is not an overarching statement about mental hospitals, just the one I was in. It was pretty shady. None of my wounds healed until I got home, meaning two entire weeks of no healing. That seems impossible, but it's what happened. I was terrified of everything: men, women, children, and even our four cats. The cats stood guard as I slept, worried for me. The only thing that helped me sleep was my parents praying over me. I was so scared and so apart from myself; there were times I'd start screaming, the memories came back of the things I saw in the dark. Or I'd dissolve into tears from what I'd gone through and bang my head against the wall from memories replaying until someone stopped me. The only thing that truly got the replaying trauma out was to write it all down, the whole experience. I lost that manuscript years ago, but I have the memories; they're just not very strong now. I relapsed into another breakdown a year later after I'd been doing so well; this time, I didn't go to the hospital. I felt better on my own, but there was nothing easy about coming back from that experience.

It's even possible I imagined the whole thing, but my family didn't. Another family member and I heard drawers opening and closing on their own upstairs, and something speaking aloud in another language, perhaps even English backwards in the room with us. Everyone saw or felt something supernatural at some point during this time, though it's not my place to share more about their experiences. It would be so much easier to believe it was extreme stress and fear due to my anxiety disorder; it would have been a relief if it were just mental illness. In my opinion, it's easier to deal with psychosis than paranormal phenomena.

My personal theory is that what entered my body was not a demon, but that demonic forces might have been involved in my oppression to break me down for possession. Naturally, I can't prove that since that assessment is based off psychic ability but some of the phenomena suggests an entity tried to manifest in the house and failed. It took me about two years total to rebuild my life after something tried to take it from me. I'm not afraid of anything paranormal now, so I guess that's a good thing to come out of this.

When I researched my thesis, I felt something dark press down on me, like a genuine psychic weight. Something doesn't want me to continue the research of demonic phenomena, but that just propelled me forward. It wasn't easy to do my research after what happened. Though I don't believe it was a demon anymore, it was still traumatic, and I had to rehash my experience. It brought back out old wounds to explain why I was interested in the subject. My advisor said what happened to me was fascinating, and I've had people tell me I'm very convincing when I tell this story aloud.

I don't ask you to believe me or any part of this book. I don't need outside validation. I went through the stages of infestation and a particularly awful oppression, but it was over a period of two weeks which is fairly quick. I think that it might have been sent after me by a dark magic practitioner, though I do not know for sure who could have done this to me or why. I have recovered fully from the possession and have little to no supernatural interference in my daily life (aside from what happens because I am psychically gifted with clairaudience, clairsentience, claircognizance, geomanticism, and a small amount of psychometry). I think that what happened to me had to do with these gifts and with mirrors being pointed at my bed for years, as I mentioned before. Something would try to access me while I slept using this mirror as a doorway. I had one propped up against a door, facing the end of my bed in the Illinois house for the entirety of us living there then I had another one in the same position in Las Vegas. It was an ordinary full-length mirror. Mirrors are thought to be portals in the occult[1]. This may or may not be true about mirrors, but I haven't had anything else happen since I took them out of the room. I may never know for sure, but I'm not alone in this experience. This brings comfort that someday I'll be able to identify it for whatever it really was.

HISTORY OF DEMONS IN ABRAHAMIC RELIGIONS

"DEMON" AND "DEVIL" TRANSLATIONS

To understand demons, one must be aware of their religious origins and how they were viewed in ancient times; demons have been in the world for an exceptionally long time. When I refer to demons as "evil," I mean both malicious towards humans and the opposite of good; their very presence causes harm to those nearby.

The Abrahamic religions of Christianity, Judaism, and Islam all mention the idea of the demon or similar evil spirits that are known for tormenting people and/or inhabiting their bodies[2]. The Greek word "daemon" was used when the Hebrew Old Testament was translated into Greek, which is the basis of the Old Testament in the Christian Bible[3]. However, this word did not necessarily mean anything negative in Greek; it simply meant "spirit" or "divine power"[4]. The negative connotation came from the Greek Old Testament that had been translated and then translated again into Latin during the Middle Ages, "diabolus," meaning "the one who divides" and "daemon" were different words at the time in Latin but merged through English then Germanic usage to have the same meaning[5]. When the Bible was translated into English in the late Middle Ages or Early Modern period, "devil" became the word used from the

Old English word "deofol," which meant "a subordinate evil afflicting humans"[6]. Today, the Standard Revised Version (RSV) and the New Standard Revised Version (NSRV) use "devil" and not "demon" in their texts. Due to translation issues, "devils" and "demons" are taken to mean the same thing, though I rarely use devil when referring to demonic entities because of the confusion it causes with The Devil, Satan.

ABRAHAMIC ANCESTRY

The three Abrahamic religions are Christianity, Islam, and Judaism; their origins are traced back to Abraham, a figure from the Bible that had a relationship with God after the Flood and the Tower of Babel[7]. Judaism came to the world from Abraham's son, Isaac, while Islam was from Abraham's other son, Ishmael[8]. These three religions have several similarities between them, but also huge schisms in belief.

CHRISTIANITY

THE FALL OF THE ANGELS

It is believed that at one point in time, there was a war in Heaven against God led by Lucifer, God's favorite angel[9]. This war ended with some angels being cast out to the earth and certain ones bound in Hell. Angels are inhuman spirits and serve God while they fight against demons in an eternal good versus evil struggle. After their defeat, the angels that lost the war became ugly and deformed through their hatred of God, becoming demons; they exist currently as servants of Satan, as Lucifer was renamed after this war[10].

DEMONS & ANGELS

Demons became associated historically with angels in the second and third centuries C.E.; before the rise of Christianity, the two were viewed as different creatures[11]. This association of the two could be an entirely made-up invention of Christians

26

from that period; there is no evidence otherwise[12]. Demons were equated with gods and demigods before Christian interpretation, and this means that fallen angels and demons could potentially be different entities; the pre-Christian Jewish and Greek worship of gods with demi-gods all fell under the umbrella of being called demons[13]. Christianity tells us that demons were once angels then pieces together the story from parts of the New Testament to back up this conglomeration of Greek and Jewish beliefs systems[14].

DEMONIC ORIGINS

Demons are also thought to have been conceived instead of having existed perpetually as once-angelic beings[15]. Within Genesis, there is a line about, "the Sons of God" (widely regarded as describing either angels or lesser deities by scholars) that depicts them lusting after then mating with humans, which lead to giant offspring called the Nephilim[16]. This story is continued in more detail in the Book of Enoch where the giants were destroyed by the Great Flood[17]. Their disembodied spirits were said to be evil and wandering the earth, making them the beginning of demons in this version[18]. The Book of Enoch explains such details about this part of Genesis; however, the Book of Enoch is not accepted in general as being part of Biblical canon but viewed as Jewish folklore[19].

ABILITIES OF DEMONS

The Christian Bible is one of the main sources of information on the abilities of the demonic. Demons can cause suicide[20], make a person sick or weak, even blind, deaf and/or mute[21]. They can cause insanity[22] and can possess people or animals[23], sometimes many at once can inhabit a body[24]. They are inhumanly strong, able to break the chains that bind them while inside a human body[25]. Demons are described as having all the abilities they had before as angels, even to appear as angels of light[26], if they were indeed angels at one point. They are said to have stores of infinite knowledge including insight to people past, present, and future, using what they know to corrupt humans through their own sins[27].

ISLAM

CREATION OF JINN

Angels were made from light, jinn were born of smokeless fire, and later, humans were created from clay; none of these beings are the same in Islam[28]. Jinn were given the free will to be good, neutral, or evil like humans were[29]. It is evil jinn, often called shaitans, marids, or ifrits (the spelling varies of these names) that Christians call demons. Iblis, a jinn elevated to the rank of angel[30] was cast out of Paradise for refusing to bow before the first human, Adam, who was made regent on Earth above him; Iblis then called to other jinn once on Earth to serve him once cast out[31].

JINN VS. GENIE

The word root that jinn derives from means "invisible, unseen, or hidden;"[32] jinn and mankind were created to worship Allah[33]. Jinn or djinn (the spelling varies) are invisible for the most part but should never be confused with genies. Genies were created from the process of global folklore and are a Westernized version of the jinn in the form that grants wishes, which comes from a story-within-a-story from *One Thousand and One Nights*[34]. Eventually, that story became mixed with jinn lore and now most people mistake them for the same entity.

JINN ABILITIES

Jinn can possess people; they eat, drink, marry, procreate, have communities, and they eventually die[35]. They tend to gather in liminal or deserted places like garbage dumps, graveyards, even bathrooms[36]. During dusk and at night is when jinn are said to be most active, so kids are usually kept inside at these times; the jinn are known shapeshifters and can take the form of black dogs or snakes[37]. At one point in time (but no longer), jinn could be used in divination because jinn could access the lowest rungs of heaven and eavesdrop on the angels' talk of the future, though the divination practice is forbidden in Islam[38]. Jinn are divided into four types: jinn, shaitan, ifrit, and marid[39].

ARE JINN DEMONS?

Jinn intrusions are normal in Middle Eastern/Islamic cultures; rites for exorcism to expel jinn exist for that reason[40]. Demons and jinn have different motivations, behaviors, and rules that bind them; in my professional opinion, I do not think they are the same entity but are often mistaken as such. The reason is because there is an overlap of similar behaviors, especially when people begin to act like animals during possessions. Jinn are shapeshifters and known for possession, but if one didn't know what a jinn was, it would probably be assumed it was a demon.

JUDAISM

Ancient Jews viewed the world around them as bustling with spirit activity; it was an accepted fact that demons and other spirits were real[41]. Spirits were also thought to interfere in people's lives, which we can tell from the numerous protection talismans, prayers, and rituals to keep one safe[42]. Demons themselves were not mentioned often in the Hebrew Bible, but that could have been due to the target audience knowing a lot about them already; it could also be from fear of speaking their power forth[43]. However, from the Second Temple to Achaemenid Persian times[44], there was massive uptick in the writings on demons[45], which is a stark contrast to preexilic Israel, a period that did not explain the origins or nature of demons at all[46]. These ancient texts come to us re-translated many times over and were reshaped from their original versions[47]. The Old Testament has been mistranslated many times, partially because Hebrew can be easy to mistranslate and then the preceding translations were into different languages[48]. Judaism was hugely influenced by surrounding cultures like Mesopotamia and Canaan, even taking on their ideas about demons[49]. This diffusion is evidenced in how many of their folk beliefs are either similar or exactly the same.

EVIL CAME FROM GOD

Evil, it was believed, came from God since He created all things, but then other texts tell us there was an external evil force out of the control of God; or, if not out of His control, then not directly acting under him[50]. These additions of evil being out of God's control were accepted later in Biblical canon. There are passages in Psalms (78:49) and Isaiah (45:7) which makes it clear that God is the creator of evil and has sent evil spirits upon people Himself. At one point in time in the Hebrew Bible, God (or the one attributed to be God) was clearly explained to be using demons for His own purposes[51]. The Old Testament God was quite different in the New Testament in the way He exerted power and punishment, so this change could be from the way the people of the time understood or wrote about God.

BECOMING EVIL

The Old Testament doesn't definitively name demons as such, but the New Testament is noticeably clear about its classification of demons[52]. By the time of the New Testament, some neutral characters became decidedly evil in folklore. Whether they were truly evil is another question. The fall happened because Satan (or Samael, often thought to be Satan) refused to bow to Adam, a story which had been circulating for about seven hundred years at least[53] and matches the story of the jinn in Islam.

Anything not of God was automatically labeled a demon for the Jewish people; *shedim* was the word used for these other once-worshipped deities and eventually *shedim* became the primary term for "demon."[54] All the gods of foreign lands were considered demons and so were perceived as being demonic–the ones mentioned by name in the Bible, anyway[55]. Once-worshipped gods–jinn etc.–are not automatically demonic, though it does tell us how the Jewish people of the time rejected or were supposed to reject all other gods. The same process happened with foreign entities and people who wanted to destroy Israelites; these groups were called Satanic at this time–in that they were associated with Satan and/or demons–so there was a lack of classification accuracy from the beginning of the Abrahamic religions[56]. Anyone, or anything, became a demon or aligned with Satan if you weren't of God, including foreign human enemies.

DEMONIC CREATION

The Talmud lists the ways demons came to be. Some were created on Sabbath Eve before the fall of the angels (who later became demons)[57] while others were "created from the wasted sperm of Adam"[58] with Lilith. Lilith was a controversial character in Judaism, explained to be Adam's first wife who was cast out for wanting to be equal to him, then Eve was created specifically from his rib to be submissive to Adam[59]. Judaism portrays Lilith as being explicitly evil[60]. In chapter five of the apocryphal Alphabet of ben Sirach, it is explained that demons come from the copulation of Lilith with Samael, or Samael and Naamah–a female demon similar to Lilith–and from Adam's sperm used by Lilith. It's also said that "souls of the wicked" become the demons of our world[61] and that people who died during the Flood that didn't go to Heaven also became demons[62]. The story of the Nephilim is also referenced as a possibility of how demons came into the world[63].

King Solomon was said in Jewish lore to have control over demonic entities which is interesting because in Islam, he had control specifically over jinn[64]. Was it jinn he had control over or demons? It's possible it was both since jinn do not appear to be the same entity as demons.

One can see the clear instances of cultural diffusion and how far folkloric ideas spread; it really comes down to what you believe. Demons do exist in other cultures, but this book is looking at demonic presences associated with Christianity primarily. I looked at all the Abrahamic religions because of this process of cultural diffusion spreading through the three religions and have it acknowledged that the Bible is an incomplete book to begin with that over time took on ideas from nearby areas.

[1] Mark Allen Peterson, "From Jinn to Genies: Intertextuality, Media, and the Making of Global Folklore." 2007.
[2] Rosemary Ellen Guiley, "The Encyclopedia of Demons and Demonology," 2009: 177.
[3] Siam Bhayro, and Catherine Rider. "Demons and Illness from Antiquity to the Early Modern Period" 2017: 81.
[4] Joseph F. Kelly 2013. "Who is Satan?: According to the Scriptures", 2013: 36.
[5] "Demon." n.d. Online Etymology Dictionary. https://www.etymonline.com/word/demon#etymonline_v_5575.
[6] "Devil." n.d. Online Etymology Dictionary. https://www.etymonline.com/word/devil.
[7] Ibid.
[8] Paul V.M. Flesher. 2016. "The Three Monotheistic Religions: Children of One Father." UW Religion Today. https://www.uwyo.edu/uw/news/2016/09/uw-religion-today-the-three-monotheistic-religions-children-of-one-father.
[9] Ibid
[10] Anthony Finlay, *Demons: The Devil, Possession & Exorcism*, 1999: 15.
[11] Ibid. 15
[12] Dale Basil Martin. "When did Angels Become Demons?" 2010: 657.
[13] Ibid. 657
[14] Ibid. 658
[15] Ibid. 658
[16] Philip C. Almond, *The Devil: A New Biography.* 2014:5.
[17] Genesis (6:2)
[18] Bhayro and Rider 2017: 84.

[19] Ibid. 84
[20] Ibid. 84 deaf and/or mute
[21] Matthew (9:33; 12:22)
[22] Matthew (4:24)
[23] Mark (5:12-13)
[24] Luke (8:2)
[25] Mark (5:4-5)
[26] 2 Corinthians (11:14)
[27] Finlay 1999: 46.
[28] El-Zein 2017: 32.
[29] Lebling 2010: 2.
[30] Ibid. 28.
[31] Ibid. 29.
[32] El-Zein 2017: xv.
[33] Quran (15:26-27)
[34] Peterson, "From Jinn to Genies", 2007.
[35] Lebling 2010: 2.
[36] Ibid. 2.
[37] Ibid. 7.
[38] Ibid. 19.
[39] Ibid. 7.
[40] Ibid. 74.
[41] Reed 2020:1.
[42] Ibid. 2.
[43] Reed 2020: 5; Kadmon 2019: 7.
[44] Reed 2020: 87.
[45] Ibid. 5.
[46] Ibid. 42.
[47] Ibid. 54.
[48] Kadmon 2019: 20.
[49] Ibid. 23.
[50] Ibid. 23.
[51] Ibid. 34-36.
[52] Ibid. 23.
[53] Ibid. 103.
[54] Ibid. 49.
[55] Ibid. 20.
[56] Ibid. 93.
[57] Ibid. 51.
[58] Ibid. 52.

[59] Jones and Flaxman 2017: Loc 868.
[60] Kadmon 2019: 116.
[61] Ibid. 53.
[62] Ibid. 54.
[63] Ibid. 133.
[64] Ibid. 58.

SIGHT

This chapter lists the different things people have seen when in the presence of the demonic; it is not as encompassing as I'd like because there are simply things that are not known or as popularly reported that demons can do. This is the most complete list that exists as a database for demonic behavior. Demons are not as mysterious or even as powerful as they want to seem; my organization of their abilities has yielded patterns of what they can and cannot do.

A common inability of a demon is to be able to appear fully human; it could be because they are so unlike us that they simply cannot appear fully human, usually around the eyes and feet, or that they do not want to, but it seems unlikely[103]. Demons can appear as angels, so it doesn't make sense that they just don't want to appear human to further manipulate us into giving them access into our lives. Once access is given, they can further torment us[104]. The goal of a demonic presence is to create fear and suffering through the manipulation of our own senses so that they can feed off it to manifest in our realm[105]. They do not exist here naturally because then everyone would see demons all the time. Manifestation takes time and energy.

Common experiences reported are the sightings of a dark, black-as-night shadow that is usually more than 5ft tall[106]. They can appear as other colors and other consistencies[107], but a huge, humanoid black shadow is the most common. Such shadows then interact with the environment around them,

35

bleeding into solid objects like walls and mirrors[108]. They also chase after people and appear as grotesque half-human, half-animal hybrids[109]. Movement within the environment is also frequent[110]; levitation, teleportation, sudden acts of invisible violence, and the materialization/dematerialization of objects are reported[111]. An example of this would be if you left money on the counter and suddenly, it was gone[112]. When dealing with a demonic presence, the object almost never materializes, especially if important in some way; if the object was religious, it might return bent or destroyed[113]. However, teleportation seems to be a trick demons pull out to mess with people, taking something important only to move it to another place you know you didn't leave it[114]. Your senses tell you you're right only to be proven wrong with what you're now seeing.

Psychic sleep is another phenomenon that is prevalent in demonic attacks; this is when the person next to you is asleep and dead to the world while you are being attacked directly[115]. You could be thrown all around the room and screaming your head off, but the person sleeping nearby doesn't wake until the attack is over. People also begin to undergo changes in their appearances and personalities because being around a demonic presence appears to have a negative effect on those nearby[116]. They become haggard, lose their youth, feel decrepit then often become angry or unstable, and depressed[117]. It is a side effect of living near a demon to have existing mental health issues amplified. People in proximity to demons will also begin to exhibit injuries ranging from scratches to stabs, burns, and gouged flesh[118]. Electrical problems will start, and people will eventually begin to see illusions[119]. I don't use the word hallucinations to describe these events because it implies that they aren't real when it's very real to the people to whom they are happening.

The legend below shows which books I pulled the narratives from and in the system itself, which pages were used if you wanted to do your own research. Remember that the check boxes next to each piece of phenomena can be used to mark which things have happened. Circle parts that seem relevant to you or underline information you find pertinent. This book is meant to be used to aid in identification for investigators and the public alike, not to sit quietly on the shelf.

LEGEND

IDP = In a Dark Place
TH = The Haunted
SH = Satan's Harvest
HLHD1 = House of Light, House of Darkness, Vol. 1
HLHD2 = House of Light, House of Darkness, Vol. 2
HLHD3 = House of Light, House of Darkness, Vol. 3
BN = Beware the Night
WDA = When Demons Attack
DC = The Devil in Connecticut

SIGHT

A. SIGHTING OF A FIGURE OR SHADOW

Nancy's three-year-old son screamed at what he called a "monster" in the middle of the night several times (BN: Page 227, 228)

Sean, the Flynn's young son, said he saw multiple occurrences of the "boogeyman" by the window (WDA: Page 16)

Doris' sons talked about the several terrifying spirits they had witnessed (WDA: Page 69)

Bobby, a young child, witnessed something that made him cry and hyperventilate in the house (WDA: Page 93)

A figure was seen levitating over a child's bed by Bob's son-in-law (WDA: Page 95); one of Bob's grandsons also witnessed the levitating figure (WDA: Page 95)

Henry saw the figure from the terrible illusion of a bethroned demon in hell at the top of the stairs (WDA: Page 142)

What she described as an "evil" spirit revealed itself to Tammy while living in an infested home (DC: Page 46)

A figure was seen by the Glatzels attacking David (DC: Page 157)

Carl Sr. had witnessed a strange figure walking around the

woods in the back of the house (DC: Page 172)

Debbie saw a figure attack David's bath; it's unclear if anyone else could see this figure (DC: Page 196)

I. COLOR

1. BLACK

Janet saw a black figure multiple times in her home (TH Loc 498, 2370)

Mary witnessed a black form a number of times (TH Loc 546, 1638, 2024, 2130)

Lorraine observed a black figure outside the Smurl house (TH Loc 1511)

Shannon watched a dark form manifest on multiple occasions (TH Loc 2136, 2789)

A relative that was visiting witnessed the dark form that the Smurls keep seeing (TH Loc 2460)

Megan spotted the dark figure the Smurls saw for a few years (TH Loc 3379)

Jack looks up and suddenly, the dark figure from their home is in the campground, staring at them (TH Loc 3051)

Jack saw the black figure in their home (TH Loc 3627)

A dark figure appeared and moved very quickly through the house (BN: Page 82)

Anne sees a black figure outside the Theriault house (SH Loc 2677)

A black shape was seen drifting around the stairs from time to time (BN: Page 36)

Jan observed figures that were darker than the dark room and surrounding night (WDA: Page 88)

Eventually, everyone in the house began to regularly see the dark figure manifest in their home (WDA: Page 94)

Arne was returning a levitating object to its place when he noticed a black figure outlined in gray (DC: Page 144)

A dark figure was often sighted after sunset in the Glatzel home (DC: Page 151)

The priests had started to be visited by black entities

repeatedly (DC: Page 218, 229)

A. SHIFTING FROM GRAY TO BLACK (OR VICE VERSA)

Stephen saw a shift of gray to black within the darkness (IDP Loc 853)

2. WHITE

Shannon woke up to a white form with big, black eyes (TH Loc 3160)

Mary noticed a white mass with pustules run past her that disappeared into the vanity (TH Loc 3644)

Luciana witnessed a white hairy creature with no eyes in her bedroom (BN: Page 28)

Janet watched a bright figure in front of her that stood in the corner of her bathroom (TH Page 148); Janet's mother also witnessed this figure later on (TH Loc 3145)

Ralph saw an unusually bright ball of light lingering in the future bride's room (BN: Page 17)

3. GOLD

Janet repeatedly observed a figure in the bathroom made of gold light (TH Loc 2354, 2401, 2407)

4. GLOWING GREEN

A glowing green apparition was witnessed at the window by a neighbor from outside (IDP Loc 3213)

II. SHADOWS / SHADOWY FIGURES

Shadows were witnessed multiple times by the entire Snedeker family at different points (IDP Loc 3655)

Other tenants complained of seeing a black shadow float upstairs (BN: Page 178)

Shadows were often seen in the McGrath house, gliding along hallways during separate encounters (WDA: Page 34)

Katie witnessed a shadow figure standing in the doorway (WDA: Page 39)

Ellie saw a shadowed figure of a man at the end of her bed (WDA: Page 40)

Jan saw shadowy figures in her home several times (WDA: Page 84, 88)

Bob witnessed a shadow figure while adjusting the house's water heater (WDA: Page 98)

Rosa observed a shadow pass by her room late at night (WDA: Page 123)

A shadow figure stared from an open closet in LaToya's room (WDA: Page 126)

Henry kept seeing shadow figures in his room at night (WDA: Page 148)

Debbie could make out a faint shadow but no one else in the family could see it aside from David (DC: Page 155)

1. PERIPHERY

Carmen witnessed a full-on figure in her periphery (IDP Loc 2531)

Stephen saw a shadow in his periphery (IDP Loc 1223)

Jan saw many black figures around her in her periphery as she did the laundry (WDA: Page 84)

2. SHADOW ANIMALS

The image of a large animal appeared as a shadow on the walls (HDHL2: Page 35)

III. WEARING CLOTHING

1. HOODED FIGURES / ROBED

The "ghost" one boy witnessed was hooded (BN: Page 178)

Kevin witnessed a hooded figure in the corner of his room;

on separate occasions, Kevin, and Holly, both saw it (WDA: Page 22, 26)

Jan and Brandon witnessed a figure wearing what looked like a monk cowl and robe (WDA: Page 83)

Bob would see a hooded figure (WDA: Page 95)

Carin noticed the dark form in a cloak in the hall (TH Loc 2425)

Brandon walked into the room where Jan was asleep and saw her being surrounded by hooded figures (WDA: Page 85-86)

Several shadow figures would crowd around Shaylee's bed that kept her awake at night (WDA: Page 114)

B. SHAPE / TEXTURE

I. FLAWED APPARITIONS

1. HUMANOID

Shannon saw a humanoid flawed apparition (TH Loc 3160, 3185)

Cindy saw an entity that looks like her sister that had black pits for eyes with distorted, horrible features, crawling things under her skin (HDHL1: Page 231)

Cindy witnessed an apparition that had a broken neck (HDHL2: Page 49)

Janet witnessed a figure shaped like a woman (TH Loc 2177)

Janet detected a human-shaped form with a cape and no features (TH Loc 498)

Cindy continually witnessed a woman figure, reporting that there were always threes on the clock and a horrible smell accompanying her visits (HDHL1: Page 206)

The figure Arne saw was a humanoid apparition that only had two dark eyes staring at him and no other features (DC: Page 144)

An apparition with arms and legs in black was on the pulpit, mimicking the priest, which was witnessed by Arne (DC: Page 230)

A. APPARITION OF DEAD PERSON / ROTTING CORPSE

Stephen and Jason both witness an apparition (IDP Loc 1728)
John sees the rotting corpse of a woman (IDP Loc 4592)
   Carolyn witnessed a human-looking but rotting apparition
(HDHL1: Page 186, 253); Annie saw the same thing (HDHL1: Page
219); Cindy also saw this same figure (HDHL2: Page 49)
   David observed a see-through apparition of a man at the
end of the waterbed after being shoved (DC: Page 22)

B. APPARITION OF FAMILIAR PERSON (TO WITNESS)

Gabby saw an apparition of her father who had died (BN: Page 23)

2. MISSING PARTS /FEATURES

Luciana spotted a white hairy creature with no eyes, laughing at her terror (BN: Page 28)

A pale disembodied arm grabbed Luciana while she was sitting in the living room (BN: Page 36)

The downstairs neighbor's child witnessed a hooded figure with huge teeth but was missing its nose (BN: Page 178)

Aubrey saw a figure sitting in a chair, but it had no features (WDA: Page 40)

The orb that transformed into a human figure had no facial features (WDA: Page 75)

Shaylee witnessed a horribly disfigured, eye-less, burned entity (WDA: Page 115)

Arne saw the entity for the first time, but only its horrible head was visible (DC: Page 156)

3. SEVERAL APPARITIONS /HORDE (FLAWED)

Several flawed apparitions appeared to the Snedekers at once (IDP Loc 4786)

Carolyn was confronted with multiple entities holding torches while she was in bed (HDHLI: Page 251)

David witnessed a horde of flawed entities that eventually crowded around his bed (DC: Page 101, 105)

The entity revealed itself to be a horde in one horrific body with changing faces and morphing shapes constantly (DC: Page 241)

4. FLAWED ANIMAL SPIRITS

A puppy that had no head or tail ran across Mary's living

room (TH Loc 798, 3155)

Chris witnessed animal-like creatures in Jan and Brandon's home (WDA: Page 88)

II. NOT SOLID: CLOUD-LIKE /GASEOUS /VAPOROUS / GELATINOUS /SHAPELESS MASS

A solid mist wearing women's clothing hovered above the floor, experienced by Cindy (HDHL1: Page 222)

A vaporous cloud-like apparition hovered over Andrea while she slept, seen by Cindy (HDHL2: Page 71)

Bob observed a dark cloud materialize that was human shaped in appearance (WDA: Page 95)

Emma and her mother both watched a dark and shadowy cloud floating in the corner (WDA: Page 118)

Sarah observed a shapeless cloud form in her room (WDA: Page 159)

The figure Aubrey witnessed wasn't fully solid and was featureless (WDA: Page 40)

Stephanie sees a shadowy, gelatinous blob several times (IDP Loc 3304, 3703)

Carmen sees a thick, dark entity swallow herself whole (IDP Loc 3692)

Father George saw a formless blob that was dark in color (IDP Loc 4479)

The entity Janet saw in bathroom was gelatinous (TH Loc 2009)

Researchers along with Kevin and Holly witnessed something rolling underneath them in a moving mass that passed under them all and under a door into the hall (WDA: Page 13)

Shapeless black masses were often seen along the halls (WDA: Page 34)

A black mass of an entity slithered into the girls' room as they watched (WDA: Page 38)

Janet watched a figure with a human-shaped figure made of rolling smoke (TH Loc 503)

Christina (who was five years old at the time) saw something wavy leaning over her sister's crib (BN: Page 94)

III. ORBS OF LIGHT

Ruth saw a white ball fly past her (BN: Page 27)
Ralph witnessed yellow orbs and black dots around Tony's head; he also saw spirit energy orbs twice (BN: Page 131)
A blue beam of light came down the chimney, making the fire go out then it proceeded to fly around the room (HDHLI: Page 243)
Orbs of light varying in size and intensity were witnessed in Doris' home (WDA: Page 72, 75)
The orbs were responsive to verbal attention and reactive when music was playing (WDA: Page 73)
The red orb David had once witnessed in his room was seen by the rest of David's family (DC: Page 158)
Carl Sr. woke up to a blue orb filling the room with light (DC: Page 171)

1. MORPHING

After the entities' chanting, a blue orb of light appeared in David's room that changed into a portal and several entities came through it (DC: Page 100-101)
The horrible face that Arne witnessed turned into an orb and disappeared shortly after (DC: Page 156)

IV. HAIRY

The entity Luciana caught sight of was a small, hairy creature (BN: Page 28)
The creature witnessed by an unnamed source had hair covering it (BN: 83)
Doug witnessed a creature with fur all over its body in the hallway (WDA: Page 34)
A hairy creature lay on Katie's bed at night (WDA: Page 36)
The hairy entity appeared in Katie and Lisa's room (WDA:

Page 38)
A large hairy creature and a small hairy creature were both witnessed by Clarita (WDA: Page 106)

V. WITH TEETH

The hairy entity had yellow teeth that it gnashed (BN: Page 83)

Cathi and Jerry separately saw the entity's "jagged, yellow teeth" in her rearview mirror (HDHLI: Page 235, 467)

Carolyn saw the same yellowed teeth in the rotting corpse that visited her among the horde (HDHLI: Page 253)

The creatures Clarita observed all had fangs (WDA: Page 106)

VI. ANIMAL SPIRITS (NON-SHADOW)

A black cat spirit prowled Ed's office (BN: Page 53)

A cat spirit ran through a door that was closed; also, the Perrons didn't have a cat (HDHLI: Page 209)

Shaylee saw an unfriendly-looking black dog on a chain accompanying the entity (WDA: Page 115)

C. MORPHING / CHANGING SHAPE

I. CORPSE TO WINGED / REPTILIAN BEAST

John observed a corpse spirit change into a winged reptile-creature (IDP Loc 4614)

11. MIST TO HUMANOID FIGURE

Janet and Jack saw the mist in their bedroom transform into a humanoid figure (TH Loc 875)

Roger witnessed an entity form from a vapor into a figure (HDHLI: Page 450)

III. ANIMAL TO SMOKY FIGURES

Shadows turned from a crow-like image into smoky figures on her wall while Cindy played (HDHL2: Page 49)

IV. ORB TO HUMANOID

The orbs at one point changed to form an image of a muscular man but only his upper half (WDA: Page 75)

Some of the orbs formed into horrendous entities in front of David (DC: Page 101-102)

D. HYBRIDS

I. ANIMAL /HUMAN HYBRID

Jack saw a half-human and half-animal hybrid (Th Loc 2201, 2704, 2810)

Janet saw a humanoid man spirit with animal horns in her home (TH Loc 2739)

Judy witnessed a hairy yet man-like creature (WDA: Page 42)

David observed a horrible human/animal hybrid entity appear to him in his room along with two others (DC: Page 66)

Some of the horde that David witnessed were human and animal hybrids (DC: Page 101-102)

II. ANIMAL /ANIMAL HYBRIDITY

E. SIZE

I. 4FT OR BELOW

Janet observed an entity that was at least 3ft tall in the bathroom (TH Loc 2009)

Mary saw an entity that was about 3ft tall (TH Loc 3644)

II. 5FT OR ABOVE

The entity that Janet witnessed was over five feet tall (Th Loc 2370)

A humanoid creature Janet saw extended higher than five feet (Th Loc 2354)

Jack witnessed a creature that was about eight feet tall (TH Loc 2704, 2810)

Brother Andrew's friend observed a creature that was at least five-feet-tall (BN: Page 83)

The figure Kevin saw in the corner was very tall (WDA: Page 22)

Katie watched a huge creature appear in front of her (WDA: Page 39)

The entity Shaylee witnessed was at least 7ft tall (WDA: Page 115)

F. INTERACTION

I. ENVIRONMENT (INTERACTION)

1. RUNNING ACROSS BED

Jack witnessed the hybrid entity run across the bed (TH Loc 2827)

2. FADING INTO SOLID OBJECTS

Mary witnessed the flawed puppy apparition without a head disappear into the couch (TH Loc 798))

Jack watched as the hybrid creature faded into the wall (TH Loc 2832, 3633)

Mary watched another flawed apparition fade into the vanity (TH Loc 3644)

Sean observed an entity pass through a wall (WDA: Page 16)

The shadow figures and shapeless masses that were seen would often fade into walls (WDA: Page 34)

The hairy entity attacking Lisa and Katie faded through a

window (WDA: Page 39)

The interactions with this entity often ended with it disappearing into the wall (WDA: Page 95)

The dark cloud faded into the wall in front of Emma and her mom (WDA: Page 118)

3. DEMATERIALIZATION OF ENTITY (VANISHING)

The monster-like creature Doug saw suddenly vanished in front of him (WDA: Page 34)

Katie watched the creature dematerialize before her eyes (WDA: Page 36)

The entity staring at Brandon eventually faded away and disappeared (WDA: Page 84, 85, 86)

David watched in horror as the apparition before him disappeared (DC: Page 22)

4. APPEARANCE THROUGH SOLID OBJECT

A. MATTRESS

Janet witnessed a human-looking hand come through the mattress (TH Loc 3100)

B. FLOOR

Debbie watched as a scaly grayish-green claw appeared through the floor right before it scratched her; Arne also witnessed this claw and had been scratched by it (DC: Page 216)

II. PEOPLE (INTERACTION)

1. BECKONING

Mary observed an entity beckon to her (TH Loc 1638)

Jack witnessed the figure beckon to him to come closer (TH Loc 3627)

2. BEING CHASED BY ENTITY

An apparition of a corpse ran down the hall at John (IDP Loc 4614)

A half-human, half-animal hybrid chased Jack down the hallways (TH Loc 2201, 2815)

3. RUDE OR THREATENING GESTURES

A. BEING FLIPPED OFF

The entity Luciana saw flipped her off (BN: Page 29)

B. MASTURBATING /HOLDING PENIS

Katie witnessed the hairy entity holding its penis in its hand (WDA: Page 36)

C. POINTING

David saw an apparition of a man who pointed at the boy threateningly (DC: Page 22)

Arne saw the entity pointing menacingly at an oak tree a few moments before he nearly crashed into it (DC: Page 161)

4. APPEARING IN MIRROR

Gabby saw an apparition within the mirror looking at her (BN: Page 9)

5. ATTACKS (WITNESSED)

David was being punched, slapped, and attacked in other ways with a new intensity (DC: Page 146)

Mary watched as Arne was tripped by something as he walked up the stairs; she saw something grab his ankle (DC: Page 141)

Judy found David being strangled by something in the living

room; right after, he was punched in the stomach right after (DC: Page 146)

Carl finally witnessed a malicious invisible force hit his son and began to believe something supernatural was happening (DC: Page 159)

David's family was forced to watch him be clubbed by invisible weapons and writhe on the floor in pain (DC: Page 193); he was also stabbed and seemingly shot (DC: Page 214)

David watched as something invisible kicked him in the stomach and his body responded (DC: Page 227)

At one point, David seemed to have experienced a heart attack: no pulse, inert, and turning white (DC: Page 242)

Jeff witnessed Ed being choked in front of him (TH Loc 1557)

Cindy couldn't breathe while immobilized by an entity (HDHLI: Page 347)

David was visibly being choked by an unseen force (DC: Page 87)

G. SEEN MOVEMENT (OR NORMAL LACK THEREOF)

I. OBJECTS

1. LEVITATION

A piece of wood lifted into the air on its own (SH Loc 2603)

Lorraine's chair was levitated by an invisible entity (TH Loc 2585)

Heavy furniture was lifted off the ground in full view of the terrified family (BN Page 26)

A can of peas was witnessed to be levitating by Luciana (BN Page 27)

Luciana's mattress was lifted into the air while she was on it (BN: Page 28)

A box of saltines was levitated towards Donna (BN: Page 275)

The phone was levitated off the hook then dropped in front of Nancy; the same thing happened to Cynthia at a different time (HDHLI: 209, 483)

Eleonore witnessed a table lift off the ground by itself (WDA:

Page 102); she also saw a table lift off the ground (WDA: Page 102)

Harry witnessed a cushion levitate off a chair (WDA: Page 104)

A piece of wood was lifted up on its own (SH Loc 2603)

A leather belt rose in the air about three feet that had been draped on the dressed in front of Debbie (DC: Page 73)

A chocolate cake lifted up from where it was sitting in full view of the Glatzels (DC: Page 143)

A makeup case levitated several times only to repeatedly hit David (DC: Page 144)

The rocking chair that had been occupied by the entity began to levitate in the Glatzel house (DC: Page 156)

The back end of the Glatzels' car was lifted up with them all in it as they tried to pay a toll (DC: Page 198)

Judy and Carl Sr.'s bed levitated about six inches high in front of Ed (DC: Page 232)

A. TILTING /SPINNING /TWISTED AROUND

A heavy trash was spun around of its own accord (TH Loc 2077)

A mattress was levitated then tilted up and down with Jack and Janet still on it (TH Loc 2386)

Barbara watched as the cigarette she'd just been smoking flipped through the air (WDA: Page 37)

The chain to the light bulb in the closet would be twisted around the bulb, no matter how many times it was unwound (WDA: Page 97)

B. FLOATING /FLYING AROUND ROOM

The Smurl children witnessed pots and pans flying around the room (TH Loc 814)

Dawn saw her earring fly around the room (TH Loc 1943)

Carolyn had a hand scythe fly directly at her in the barn (HLHDI: Page 99)

Luciana had a glass thrown at her head that barely missed her (BN: Page 21)

An ashtray was thrown across one of the bedrooms in the Villanova house (BN: Page 28)

Luciana's bed and chairs would fly around her room (BN: Page 27)

Several objects flew around the room, terrorizing the Villanovas (BN: Page 36)

Jill's entire closet came flying out as if being thrown (BN: Page 75)

Cindy's possessions were thrown all around the room while she looked on, clinging to her mattress for dear life (HDHL1: Page 435)

Cindy and Lori watched helplessly as objects began to fly around the room (HDHL1: Page 23)

Cindy and her friend Joyce witnessed an axe seemingly thrown at Cindy (HDHL2: Page 58)

Roger touched a pot on the stove, and it flew off the stove and fell near his feet (HDHL2: Page 235)

Sticks that had been holding up windowsills up flew across the room, witnessed by Keith, Cindy, and Nancy (HDHL2: Page 327)

Andrea's boombox was thrown across the kitchen, which Cindy saw (HDHL3: Page 23)

A frying pan flew out of the cabinet by itself, floated for a bit in a circle then hit the ground (WDA: Page 70)

Poster boards were torn from the ceiling and thrown across the room (WDA: Page 77)

Bottles of ink were thrown across Eleonore's room (WDA: Page 103)

A steel letter opener was thrown across the room in front of scientists while testing Eleonore (WDA: Page 105)

A bottle of air freshener was thrown into LaToya's bedroom, witnessed by everyone (WDA: Page 126)

Teacups had a habit of flying cross the room in front of Sarah and Justin (WDA: Page 163)

Arne's cross flew across the room and hit Debbie on her forehead (DC: Page 202)

53

2. TELEPORTATION OF OBJECTS
(MOVED FROM ONE PLACE TO ANOTHER)

A. INSTANTANEOUS

Objects were moved around the Snedeker house multiple times (IDP Loc 3655, 4371, 4376, 4635)

The countess observed things teleported from the air rain down (WDA: Page 103)

Harry witnessed a mirror be teleported from one room to another (WDA: Page 104)

B. UNNOTICED OR UNSEEN

Carmen laid out plates and silverware only to come back and find them moved back where it previously was (IDP Loc 1089)

Carmen loses her purse and finds it in Stephen's room, where she didn't leave it (IDP Loc 1531)

Tools were gone then appeared back where they had been left previously (BN: Page 225)

Ginny put her clothes in the washer and when she came back down, the heavy washing machine was turned completely around (BN: Page 227)

Cindy's toys were moved unnaturally fast when she left the room (HDHLI: Page 208)

Nancy's things would be moved in her room when she came back (HDHLI: Page 208)

Toys and tools left in the barn would go missing that then appeared in the house (HDHLI: Page 211)

While they slept, Roger and Carolyn's bed moved halfway across the room; neither noticed until awake (HDHLI: Page 229, 255)

The Perron girls' possessions would be constantly moved, causing discord among the siblings (HDHLI: Page 375)

Cindy would come home to have her bedroom's furniture completely moved to opposite ends of the room (HDHLI: Page

432)

Nancy had her diary moved from the place she left it while no one was home (HDHLI: Page 460)

The phone would forever be off the hook in the Flynn household when it wasn't left that way (WDA: Page 16)

Photos of the Flynns' children were facing the wall when they came downstairs one morning (WDA: Page 26)

Doris' sons noticed how objects would shift around the house (WDA: Page 69)

Objects in Jan's house would be moved mysteriously (WDA: Page 83)

All of the photos on Jan's bedside table were facing down, though an hour previously, they were facing the right way (WDA: Page 85)

Personal items in the house would end up in places they weren't put originally (WDA: Page 94)

Furniture in Bob and Lesa's house would shift on its own (WDA: Page 94)

A toy from Charlie's childhood ended up in a space that had been closed up since 1910 (WDA: Page 97)

Nuns had their habits moved from one room to another, which were behind locked doors (WDA: Page 102)

Small objects were moved around the house and ended up in strange places they weren't left (WDA: Page 157)

The lawn chair that had previously been folded up in the yard was now open, as if someone was sitting there (DC: Page 51)

The air-conditioning in the Glatzel house had been turned off behind locked doors that no one in the family had touched (DC: 60)

When Arne tried to get out of a car that was coming to life even though it was turned off, he found the door locked (DC: Page 161)

3. FORCIBLE /VIOLENT MOVEMENT (OBJECTS)

A. THROWN /SHOVED

Lorraine's chair was smashed into a table (TH Loc 2585)

Luciana's possessions were thrown and slammed around the room (BN Page 26)

A tissue box and a can of peas were thrown at Luciana (BN: Page 27)

The countess witness furniture moving on its own; items were moved from one room to another (WDA: Page 103)

Ruth had a soap dish hurled at her (BN Page 27)

Luciana's mattress was tossed to the floor (BN: Page 28)

In front of witnesses, a seashell tree was pitched off the mantel (BN: Page 229)

Judy's cosmetics and perfumes had been knocked over on her dresser a few times (DC: Page 75, 96)

The mattress stored in Kate's basement was randomly thrown from the wall it was resting on to the middle of the floor (DC: Page 85)

B. SLAMMED /FLUNG

When Cindy would try to go through a room, the doors would slam in her face (HDHL1: Page 209)

The woodshed door was flung twenty feet away (HDHL2: Page 175)

The windows that had been held open a moment ago slammed down by themselves violently (HDHL2: Page 327)

Cindy had her four-poster bed frame hit the wall, the floor, and flying around the room while she was levitated on her mattress (HDHL3: Page 170)

Harry watched as books were pushed off a shelf (WDA: Page 104)

Liam witnessed Sarah's wardrobe be propelled from the wall and fall onto the bed where he'd just been laying (WDA: Page 161)

Books were shoved off the shelf by invisible hands (WDA: Page 162)

C. VIOLENT PUNCHING OF OBJECTS (REPEATED)

The Smurl children witnessed their pillows punched violently by something invisible (TH Loc 814)
The Smurl van was struck by invisible hands (Th Loc 2194)

D. VIOLENT MOORINGS /LATCH/HANDLE PHENOMENA

A heavy brass chandelier was swinging violently overhead (BN: Page 166)
The chandelier became dislodged from the ceiling plaster in response to holy words spoken aloud (BN: Page 166)
The woodshed door was torn off its hinges (HDHL2: Page 175)
The Smurl family and Ed observed the mirror on the dresser being ripped from screws that held it down (TH Loc 1159)

I. OBJECT TORN FROM WALL /CEILING

Poster boards were ripped off of Doris' bedroom walls (WDA: Page 75)
The light in Smurl duplex crashed down from ceiling, nearly landing on Janet and the girls (TH Loc 597)
A nailed wooden board was torn from the wall and thrown across the room, almost hitting one of Doris' sons (WDA: Page 76)

E. OBJECT YANKED ON /TUGGED ON (WITNESSED)

Maurice had a cross yanked out of his hand, witnessed by others (SH Loc 2288)
A chair was visibly pulled out from Roger on its own; it happened to everyone else as well (HDHL1: Page 212-213, 309)
The cigarette Barbara had been smoking was taken from

her mouth by an invisible force (WDA: Page 37)

Cups would topple over on their own in the house (WDA: Page 94)

The Bible Arne reached for slid away from his reach (DC: Page 154)

F. OBJECTS BROKEN /RUINED

China from the hutch fell out and broke (TH Loc 2350)

Objects that flew around the Theriault house broke on impact (SH Loc 2557)

Family pictures had been destroyed nearby Luciana (BN: Page 27)

A soap dish that was thrown smashed into the wall and broke on impact (BN Page 27)

The light violently hit the ceiling and crystals rained down in the room from the broken chandelier (BN: Page 166)

Nina had to watch as her possessions in the house were knocked around and habitually destroyed (BN: Page 167)

A teacher had her glass shower door break inward, as if something had slammed into it (BN: Page 172)

Carolyn noticed her entire knot of twine had been shredded sometime during the night (HDHL1: 140)

Fragile items would continually be broken in the house (WDA: Page 94)

The rainfall of rocks that rained down on the house broke windows in Eleonore's house (WDA: Page 102)

Windows shattered, causing shards to fall inside and outside Eleonore's house (WDA: Page 102)

Eleonore's books and personal items were torn up or ruined by invisible hands (WDA: Page 103)

LaToya's bedside table lamp was broken by a thrown bottle of air freshener (WDA: Page 126)

Cindy's previously indestructible music player was broken (HDHL3: Page 21)

The chocolate cake the Glatzels had planned to eat rose in the air and was smeared on a kitchen cabinet then slid to the ground (DC: Page 143)

David's birthday cake was ruined by the entities (DC: Page 198)

I. CLAW MARKS

A newly remodeled bathroom was destroyed by claw marks (TH Loc 351)

The woodwork and trim were also found to be clawed (TH Loc 351)

Pictures of Brandon were discovered with his face scratched out (WDA: Page 85)

II. SHREDDING

One of the Smurl's bedspreads had been shredded by what looked like claws (TH Loc 860)

G. RELIGIOUS OBJECT TARGETED

Ralph's St. Dominic medal fell off its string, though it was unbroken (BN: Page 7)

A crucifix was put in Nancy's son's room, and it was found on the floor the next morning with the nail still in the wall (BN: Page 229)

The Bible was found thrown in the middle of the room, opened to Isaiah 28 each time (noted at least three times) (WDA: Page 16, 19)

A crucifix and a framed picture of Christ was broken in the Flynn home (WDA: Page 29)

The Cranmers found a crucifix bent into the shape of an L (WDA: Page 94)

Crucifixes would be broken from rosaries, crosses thrown across the room, religious jewelry yanked off necks while in the Cranmer residence (WDA: Page 96, 98)

Ryan watched as a crucifix bent in front of him (WDA: Page 97)

Sarah witnessed the entity take her painting of Christ off the hooks and throw it to the ground, which broke it (WDA: Page 160)

Ralph's St. Dominic medal fell off its string, though it was unbroken (BN: Page 7)

Barbara's favorite angel sculpture had been thrown to the floor and broke (WDA: Page 37)

One of the holy candles being used by Glatzels was thrown across the room, splashing red wax on the wall (DC: Page 96)

I. HOLY WATER TURNING BROWN

Investigators watched as holy water turned brown on them (BN: Page 36)

II. IMAGE OF JESUS TORN

Jesus' image was torn off a rosary (BN: Page 36)

4. MISCELLANEOUS OBJECT MOVEMENT

Alan and Jason wanted to sleep in the living room because they heard strange noises in their closet (DC: Page 86)

A. VIBRATION /RATTLING /RIFFLING THROUGH

Al observed the bed vibrating of its own accord (IDP Loc 1653)

Objects in the Snedeker house began to rattle on the shelves (IDP Loc 4571)

Knickknacks in Smurl house vibrated (TH Loc 1905)

Jack and Janet's mattress started vibrating randomly (Th Loc 2343)

A vase rattled in the Smurl household with nobody touching it (TH Loc 3393)

Objects would rattle in Theriault house (SH Loc 1703)

Furniture began to shake as if from an earthquake that wasn't occurring (BN Page 26)

Jen awoke to the   rattling, as if someone were trying to get in (BN: Page 245)

The Flynn's Bible was seen being riffled through by something invisible (WDA: Page 24)

The stomping in the attic was so bad that it vibrated throughout the Glatzel house (DC: Page 58)

B. APPEARANCE OF BREATHING /LIFE

A toy walked across an unnamed boy's room by itself (BN: Page 54)

Cindy saw her blankets appear to breathe (HDHLI: Page 439)

A plastic doll not made to cry began to cry in front of Doug when he walked into Lisa's room (WDA: Page 34)

A dinosaur toy appeared to come to life, walking towards David when he'd come into the kitchen for a glass of water (DC: Page 98)

I. DEPRESSION IN MATTRESS (INVISIBLE)

Everyone present in the Snedeker residence at the time witnessed the mattresses appearing to breathe (IDP Loc 4376)

Cindy would continually see indentations on her mattress from something invisible (HDHLI: Page 439)

C. ROCKING BACK AND FORTH

A chain moving back and forth in basement that had no discernible source of movement (IDP Loc 4392)

The TV in Jack and Janet's room began to rock back and forth (TH Loc 3543)

All the laundry on the line at Smurls' campsite flew off the line without any kind of wind blowing (TH Loc 2053)

An unoccupied chair began to rock back and forth as if someone was sitting in it (DC: Page 75, 155, 232)

D. MANIPULATION OF OBJECT

I. REARRANGED IN SHAPE

Pictures on the walls would be rotated of their own accord (WDA: Page 94)

CROSS

Luciana's flowers were taken from her vase and rearranged into a cross shape (BN: Page 26)

FIGURE EIGHT

Bob found the light chain twisted into the shape of a figure eight (WDA: Page 98)

E. OBJECTS FALLING UNNATURALLY

A cloth heart fell from Donna's kitchen when Mike asked the entity to move something (BN: Page 269)
The Bible would fall randomly to the floor, always opened to the same passage (WDA: Page 18, 21)
A cross fell when the nail should have held it onto the wall in front of Liam (WDA: Page 160)

5. MATERIALIZATION (APPEARS FROM NOWHERE)

A. SEMEN (INHUMAN)

B. WATER

Eleonore's shoes would fill up with water that had no discernable source (WDA: Page 103)

C. SAND

Sand appeared on the basement floor, about two buckets worth (WDA: Page 123)

D. BLOOD

Something that resembled bloody streaks would appear high up on the walls of specific rooms (WDA: Page 94); the blood-looking streaks eventually turned into splatters on the walls (WDA: Page 95)

The walls began to bleed without a source (WDA: Page 97)

The floors appeared to bleed when they were cleaned in the Smurl house (IDP Loc 1007)

Blood appeared from nowhere on Maurice's shirt (SH Loc 3308)

Maurice's eyes began to bleed suddenly (SH Loc 194, 965, 3257, 3308, 3615)

Maurice's mouth and nose were bleeding of their own accord (SH Loc 3572, 3615)

E. GREASE/OIL

Mary Smurl had purchased a new carpet that suddenly had a large, round grease stain (TH Page 22)

F. ROCKS

Rocks have fallen on houses like hail in various other cases (BN: Page 36)

Eleanore had rocks fall on her house like rain (WDA: Page 102)

6. VANISHMENT/DEMATERIALIZATION OF OBJECTS (NEVER RECOVERED)

Carmen bought two six-packs of soda, put them in fridge and they promptly vanished (IDP Loc 1611)

A St. Jude medal was taken from Jack's neck while he slept (TH Loc 780)

Dawn's makeup was taken from her bureau (TH Loc 1319)

Dawn's clothes vanished, which caused discord between her and Kim (TH Loc 1941)

Mary's pots and pans on the other side of the duplex were disappearing (TH Loc 2007)

Luciana's Blessed Mother medallion disappeared while she was sleeping (BN Page 20)

Ralph's card disappeared and was never recovered within Nancy's house (BN: 229)

Objects in the Perron household would never be seen again once they disappeared (HDHL1: Page 375)

Keys and cups would go missing in Flynn house (WDA: Page 16)

Things that disappeared were never recovered in Bob and Lesa's house (WDA: Page 94)

7. MANIPULATION OF PHYSICS LAWS

Roger threw a cigarette out of his car window that then somehow passed through the closed glass backdoor window and landed on Cindy; Cindy witnessed this happen (HDHL1: Page 340)

A. IMPOSSIBLE BALANCING OF OBJECTS

Theriault household saw a tray with four cups balanced on top of a curtain rod (SH Loc 2924)

B. RUNNING INTO AN UNSEEN WALL

Ralph's dog ran into an invisible wall (BN: Page 244-245)

Doris and her sons experienced being run into by something invisible/them running into it (WDA: Page 69)

C. MYSTERIOUS WEIGHT

Cindy couldn't open a box that she was inside even though there was no latch and nothing holding it down (HDHL2: Page 53)

D. SHOULD HAVE BROKEN FROM IMPACT

Andrea's boombox was thrown across the room with enough force to break it, but there wasn't a scratch on it (HDHL3: Page 23)

E. BOUNCING (PEOPLE)

David's body was bounced up and down for half an hour very quickly by the entities (DC: Page 198)

8. FIRES /EXPLOSIONS /SINGEING /SCORCHING

An iron pot exploded in Eleonore's house (WDA: Page 102)
Nancy's black notebook was found charred (SH Loc 1622)
Smurls had unexplained fires around their duplex, multiple instances with their TV, oven, and car (TH Loc 338)
Mysterious fires broke out on Maurice's farm several times (SH Loc 1690, 1718, 3007, 3033)
A rubber ball burst into flame that hung from Carl's rearview mirror (BN: Page 29)
A toy's head violently exploded off its body, shattering it upon impact (BN: Page 54)
The edges of all the Perron children's blankets were singed by fire when they awoke (HDHL1: Page 232)
Carolyn saw flames in her bedroom several times (HDHL1: Page 254)

9. UNSEEN HAND WRITINGS (WITNESSED)

A. MIRRORS

Ed saw gossamer threads form words on a mirror (TH Loc 1568- 1573)

I. ENGLISH BACKWARDS

Ruth and other members of the family found the word 'help' was written backwards on the mirror several times (BN: Page 27)

II. PROFANITIES

III. OTHER LANGUAGES

II. PEOPLE (MOVEMENT AROUND PEOPLE)

1. LEVITATION

Mary Smurl's mattress was levitated with her on it (TH Loc 895)

Jack and Janet's mattress was levitated while they were still on it (Th Loc 2345)

LaToya's granddaughter was witnessed levitating while unconscious (WDA: Page 124

A priest watched as Eleonore sat on a trunk then it immediately began rocking up and down (WDA: Page 102)

Jack and Janet mutually felt his bed levitate from its frame (TH Page 148)

A. BUMPING INTO WALLS

Janet was levitated then bumped into walls (TH Loc 2683)

Maurice was bouncing off the walls by an unseen force (SH Loc 2744)

B. TWISTED AROUND (MIDAIR)

The oldest son was flipped around midair (WDA: Page 126)

C. HURLED ACROSS ROOM /TO FLOOR (FROM MIDAIR)

Jack was levitated then hurled onto the floor (TH Loc 2019)
Janet was hurled across the room (TH Loc 2683)
After being twisted around, the boy was thrown off the porch (WDA: Page 126)
The youngest boy was lifted into the air and thrown into a nearby wall (WDA: Page 127)

D. SHAKEN FROM MIDAIR

Cindy's bed was lifted up and shaking, as if it were trying to throw her onto the floor (HDHL1: Page 435, 438), (HDHL3: Page 169, 170)

2. IMMOBILIZATION OF ANOTHER (WITNESSING THEIR INABILITY TO MOVE)

Janet witnessed Jack being immobilized (TH Loc 738)
Chris saw Janet was unable to move by an unseen force (TH Loc 1820)

3. PSYCHIC SLEEP

Al did not wake up when Carmen shook him roughly while activity had started (IDP Loc 3799)
Chris was still asleep when John tried to wake her up (IDP Loc 4570)
Jack couldn't awaken when Janet tried to rouse him (TH Loc 875, 2689)
Janet didn't wake when Jack tried awaken her (TH Loc 1379, 2832)
Roger didn't wake no matter what Carolyn did (HDHL1: Page 186, 252)
Justin didn't wake while Sarah was next to her, even as she was being sexually assaulted by the entity (WDA: Page 157)
The stomping in the attic should have been enough to wake Carl but curiously, he didn't awaken though Alan did (DC: Page

4. OBJECT ATTACKING PERSON (DIRECT)

A piece of wood was thrown by an invisible entity and hit Maurice in the head (SH Loc 2603)

Carolyn had a hanger attack her neck and shoulders of its own accord (HLHD1: Page 106)

Luciana was hit with on her head with a shoe (BN: Page 28)

Cindy and Lori repeatedly experienced objects hitting their bodies in a tornado of supernatural phenomena (HDHL2: Page 24)

Nancy was hit by an unidentified object, which knocked her to the ground (HDHL2: Page 327)

Two candelabras flew across the room, hitting Doris on the arm (WDA: Page 76)

Eleanore watched as small objects in the house began to fall on her (WDA: Page 102)

A friend of Eleonore's was hit in the head by a flying spoon (WDA: Page 102)

Fritz witnessed Eleonore hit in the face by a saltshaker from her table (WDA: Page 103)

Rosa's granddaughter was hit in the head with an unattached headboard (WDA: Page 127)

Maurice felt the Christmas lights strangling him (SH Page 156)

Debbie was hit on her forehead with a silver cross (DC: Page 202)

5. OBSERVING PERIPHERAL MOVEMENT

Carmen saw something move in her periphery (IDP Loc 2526)

Snedeker family often witnessed things in their periphery rushing by them (IDP Loc 3655)

Ed and Lorraine would observe things move from periphery (IDP Loc 4376)

III. ANIMALS /INSECTS (MOVEMENT)

1. LEVITATION

The Smurl's dog was levitated in front of them (TH Loc 1638)

2. TELEPORTATION

Janet witnessed the dog be teleported (TH Loc 1651)
Kevin and Holly ran from the hooded figure in their room only to be confronted with it waiting for them instantaneously at the bottom of the stairs (WDA: Page 23)
Janet had chained the family dog outside then somehow found him in the living room (TH Loc 2009)

3. MYSTERIOUS ILLNESS /BODY PROBLEM (ANIMALS)

A. CONVULSIVE TWITCHING

The Smurl's dog was convulsively twitching (TH Loc 794)

4. OUTDOOR ANIMALS APPEARING INDOORS

A. FLIES

Snedekers often saw flies in the house (IDP Loc 3719)
The Perrons had infestations of flies throughout the winter (HLHD1: 83, 134, 160), (HDHL3: Page 210)
In the middle of winter, flies would swarm LaToya's home (WDA: Page 123)
The Glatzel house began to have a problem with flies manifesting inside the house that didn't behave like normal flies (DC: Page 142)

5. STRANGE PET OR ANIMAL BEHAVIOR

Pineridge the horse became suddenly terrified in front of Nancy out of nowhere by something she couldn't see (HDHL2:

Page 186)

A. CONTINUALLY IN ATTACK MODE

A random dog mysteriously shows up at night to bark at Snedeker residence (IDP Loc 2016, 2033, 2190)

The dogs would bark continuously when it got dark on the Theriault property (SH Loc 3150)

A kitten was in attack mode, hissing at something invisible and moved sideways in a strange way (BN: Page 63)

Ralph's dog began to bark and growl like crazy after phenomena (BN: Page 244)

The Perron dogs, Jennifer and Pooh Bear continually freaked out during the random attacks on their people and the house (HDHL1: Page 309), (HDHL2: Page 172, 196, 443)

Pepper would be constantly in attack mode, barking and growling at the basement door (DC: Page 141)

B. DRAWN TO SPECIFIC PLACES

The Smurls' dog was drawn to their closet (TH Loc 3130)

Pepper, the dog, was drawn to the basement door for no explainable reason (DC: Page 141)

C. ODD AGITATION /WHINING

One dog became very agitated as the exorcism began (BN: Page 33)

Ralph witnessed a few cases where demonic phenomena got every dog in the neighborhood to howl (BN: Page 64)

The Perrons' dog was whining and cowering after the family found the cellar doors open by themselves (HDHL1: Page 228)

Pepper would whine at the basement door and growl, clearly threatened by something behind the door (DC: Page 141)

D. CONSTANT HIDING

The Perrons' cat was usually hiding behind the sofa,

seemingly from something (HDHL1: Page 228)

E. REFUSAL TO COME INSIDE /STAY INSIDE

A cat the Perrons had adopted had to go to a neighbor because it wouldn't stay inside the house (HDHL2: Page 443)

IV. OUTDOOR PHENOMENA HAPPENING INDOORS

1. MIST INSIDE HOUSE /VAPOR

A mist filled Janet and Jack's bedroom then happened again a few nights later (TH Loc 875, 2734)
Christ saw vapor come out of his mouth in a room that read seventy degrees on the thermometer (TH Loc 1820)
Steam came out of Janet's mouth while Jack was looking at her (TH Loc 2412)

H. CHANGES WITHIN PEOPLE
(INFESTATION & OPPRESSION STAGES)

I. HAGGARD OR UGLINESS TO FEATURES
(NOT PRESENT BEFORE)

Carmen and Laura looked haggard to Father George when he visited (IDP Loc 4464)
Luciana's under-eye bags were very dark (BN: Page 27)
Carolyn started to look shriveled and unrecognizable (HDHL1: Page 290)
Everyone in the Glatzel family had the same weary, haggard look (DC: Page 162)

1. SUDDEN LACK OF HYGIENE

Stephen's hygiene got worse suddenly (IDP Loc 2051)

2. CHANGE IN EYES /VOICE

Stephen's eyes no longer seemed familiar to his mother (IDP Loc 2502)
Al also noticed a change in Steven's eyes (IDP Loc 2653)
Carolyn's voice became hollow and shrill, unlike her deeper normal voice (HDHL1: Page 290)

3. PUFFINESS IN FEATURES

Carmen and Laura's faces looked puffy (IDP Loc 4464)

4. REPTILIAN FEATURES

Stephen looked reptilian in his features at times, noted by his mother (IDP Loc 1906)

5. ACCELERATED AGING /DIMINISHED VITALITY

Carolyn began to age rapidly while in the house (HDHL1: 196, 290), (HDHL2: Page 341, 392, 459)
Chrissy seemed to have aged after an entity seemingly used her body like a ventriloquist to scare her sister, Cindy (HDHL1: Page 232)

I. PHOTOGRAPHY /VIDEO ISSUES

I. APPEARANCE OF FIRE (IN PHOTO)

In a photograph taken of him, there were flames that shouldn't be there (SH Loc 2778)

II. BLEACHING OF PHOTO (COMPLETELY WHITE)

Photos were taken of Doris' house, and many came out completely white, capturing nothing (WDA: Page 71-72); another picture was taken in the same session that only bleached

Candy's face (WDA: Page 72)

III. FACES

In a photo of the basement stairs, what looks like a face can be seen (WDA: Page 133)

IV. ORBS/SPIRIT FORMS (PHOTOGRAPHY)

Orbs and crude spirit forms had begun to show up in the family polaroids (DC: Page 151)

J. ELECTRICAL PROBLEMS & APPLIANCE REPAIR ISSUES

The electrical bills in the Perron house reflected a spike in electrical use that no one could explain (HDHL1: Page 217)
All of the girls' electric blankets were burned without having been plugged in (HDHL1: Page 233)
Electrical items in the house would often randomly stop working, usually without a discernible reason (WDA: Page 162)

I. TURNING ON AND /OR OFF

Electrical appliances would habitually turn on by themselves (WDA: Page 162)

1. LIGHT FIXTURE PHENOMENA

A. ON/OFF, FLICKERING, BRIGHTENING /DIMMING

Carmen witnessed the lights turn off after something rubbed against her and the room turned cold (IDP Loc 1443)
The lamp started to flicker, almost blacking out completely (IDP Loc 3833)
Lights periodically flickered on and off in the Smurl duplex (TH Loc 571)

The lights in Ralph's apartment would flicker on and off on their own (BN: Page 66)

Lights would go on and off in Jan and Brandon's apartment (WDA: Page 86)

The lights in Bob and Lesa's house flickered on and off (WDA: Page 94)

At one point, Donna's kitchen was suddenly filled with flashing lights (BN: Page 270)

The lights would dim suddenly then brightening and dim again (SH Loc 2924)

The TV turned on so brightly that Jack and Janet had to look away because the brightness caused pain (TH Loc 1272)

The lights dimmed in response to Debbie challenging the entity to dim the lights then flashed three times (DC: Page 77)

Square flashing lights appeared on dark walls in the Glatzel home (DC: Page 213-214)

B. LIGHTS ON (WITHOUT BULBS) /NOT PLUGGED IN

Light woke up Michael when the bulbs were taken out of the room by Al (IDP Loc 2421)

Smurl's TV set was giving off an eerie glow when unplugged (TH Loc 1165)

C. UNNATURAL LIGHTS OR COLORING

Jenny and others saw the bark of an elm tree glowing for days (SH Loc 1713, 1718)

Other objects started to glow in the dark (SH Loc 1718)

A red light filled the center of the room while David was being spoken to and threatened by an invisible entity (DC: Page 66)

2. TV

The TV turned on by itself when Benjamin and Jessica had left the room (SH Loc 3075)

The TV would blare at night, turning itself on (BN: Page 27)

3. TELEPHONE ISSUES

A. RINGING PHENOMENA

The Smurls' phone rang repeatedly (TH Loc 2723)

Carolyn and Roger both tried to answer the phone, but it kept ringing even when it was taken off the hook (HDHLI: Page 332, 381)

Carolyn unplugged the phone from the wall, and it still rang; Roger pulled out the wires as well (HDHLI: Page 332)

B. UNABLE TO HEAR FROM STATIC /BEEPING /CRACKLING

Mike kept having his conversation interrupted by static then eventually disconnected (BN: Page 261, 271)

Donna had incessant beeping on her phone (BN: Page 263, 271)

Roger would pick up the phone but hear nothing but static on the other end or a strange crackling sound (HDHLI: Page 381)

4. JOINTS /PLUMBING ISSUES

Carmen had found the faucet in bathroom running, emitting scalding water and steam (IDP Loc 1605)

Smurls had consistent plumbing problems in the house (TH Loc 347)

All the joints leaked in the Smurl duplex, even after they had been fixed (TH Loc 343)

An unplugged washing machine flooded the basement at one point (DC: Page 214)

5. CAR

Donna's car battery died when she tried to leave the house; jumpstarting it did nothing (BN: Page 273)

Mike had a full tank of gas and after driving twenty miles, it was suddenly empty (BN: Page 280)

Arne lost control of the car and couldn't brake or stop it at all though the brake lights were on (DC: Page 161)

6. COMPUTER

Computers in the house would freeze often in the Cranmer house, making work impossible (WDA: Page 96)

7. CLOCK PHENOMENA

Clocks would regularly just stop working for no apparent reason for the Cranmers (WDA: Page 96)
Carmen's alarm didn't go off when she was sure it was set for the next day (IDP Loc 1516)

K. LACK OF LIGHT /DARKNESS CHANGES /GRIMINESS

I. EVER-PRESENT DARKNESS
(EVEN IN DIRECT SUNLIGHT)

Carmen couldn't get natural light to come into the house even though it faced the sun (IDP Loc 497, 669)
Father Nolan noticed the ever-present darkness in house (IDP Loc 4683)

1. SUDDEN TOTAL DARKNESS

A relative was plunged suddenly into total darkness while using the bathroom (TH Loc 2460)

2. GENERAL GRIMINESS OF PLACE /DULLNESS /UNABLE TO BE POLISHED OR REMOVED FULLY

Judy had worked on getting one of the rooms clean for most of the afternoon but had only managed to get the dirt off some objects; there was a general dark haziness to all objects in the room (DC: Page 23)
White paint turned a dirty brown only after a week (BN:

L. ILLUSIONS

I. UGLY/STRANGE IMAGES PROJECTED

Stephen started to see ugly and violent images in his mind (IDP Loc 2813)

Al saw a mutilated Christ on the cross that was horrific in appearance (IDP Loc 4168)

Lorraine saw images in her head of corpses (IDP Loc 4716)

Carmen was trapped in a deep hole illusion and she also experienced a long road with spirit blobs (IDP Loc 4231-4268, 4290)

While being physically attacked by the entity, Ellie's mind was filled with horrible, sick thoughts from the entity (WDA: Page 40)

Henry saw hell and a Satan-like figure with winged demons sitting on a throne (WDA: Page 141)

David could see that the apparition of the old man had changed into a hideous monster (DC: Page 32)

1. FACES

Jack saw his own face in a mirror, badly decomposed (TH Loc 3453)

A face imprinted itself on the Villanovas' dining room ceiling (BN: Page 35)

Cindy witnessed Chrissy's face change into something twisted and evil before her eyes (HDHLI: Page 347)

Serena saw the faces of the men in front of her change into awful, ugly features (WDA: Page 58)

The entity projected its inhuman face onto the wall for Carl Sr. to see and smiled evilly at him (DC: Page 171)

The entity's face was projected on all the Glatzel family photos (DC: Page 214)

A. FRAGMENTATION /WAVY

Judy looked around and all the furniture looked wavy to her (WDA: Page 34); the same thing happened to Aubrey later when she looked around her room (WDA: Page 41)

2. ANIMAL PARTS

A. SKULLS

An animal skull was imprinted onto a basement mirror (BN: Page 36)

B. HOOVES

Serena witnessed the illusion of animal hooves on men instead of feet (WDA: Page 58)

II. FOOTPRINTS PHENOMENA

Nancy noticed Maurice had no discernible footprints that should have been there (SH Loc 1562)

Angelo saw no tracks in the snow when there should have been because she heard someone walking (BN: Page 64)

Wet boot prints were seen by Rosa that looked like they originated in the basement (WDA: Page 123)

1. HOOVES

Sooty hoofprints were left on Judy's white bedspread in her room that then faded as the priest came into the room (DC: Page 96)

III. ROOM TILTING

Everyone in the Smurl house at the time observed the entire room tilt (IDP Loc 4762)

IV. DOPPELGANGER /BI-LOCATION APPEARANCE

The appearance of two Maurices were present multiple times (SH Loc 228, 922, 1556, 1567, 2576, 3139, 3476)

V. BLOODY ILLUSIONS

Carmen sees the floor and mop bucket suddenly change to blood (IDP Loc 1007-1013)

Blood seemingly appeared on the floor to Al/Stephanie/Peter/Michael while Carmen mopped (IDP Loc 2697)

Maurice watched himself bleed from a wound that wasn't there (SH Loc 1685)

A ridiculous amount of blood gushed somehow from an orange all over Carolyn (HDHL1: Page 491)

Cindy witnessed blood-streaked walls while down in the well on her family's property (HDHL2: Page 116)

1. RELIGIOUS ASSOCIATION

Crucifixes appeared to drip blood when Maurice was near (SH Loc 858, 876, 882, 1718)

VI. INJURY OR DISAPPEARANCE OF INJURY (NOT TRULY THERE)

Maurice would appear to be injured but unharmed in actuality (SH Loc 1685, 1724)

Scratches disappeared that were on Maurice's back (SH Loc 2912)

David's stab wounds should have been bleeding, but the only evidence were thin red lines and a lingering soreness (DC: Page 105, 121)

Carmen's throat swelled up, turned black, which appeared injured (IDP Loc 4219, 4332)

David's head looked like it was forced 180 degree around until he was looking backwards (DC: Page 175)

Maurice had the shape of a cross slashed into his back
(SH Loc 206, 2316, 2894)

VII. MATERIALIZATION (NOT THERE)

1. FIRE/SMOKE PHENOMENA

The Snedekers watched smoke rise from the carpet that

reached for them (IDP Loc 4774)

Carolyn saw her bedroom dresser burst into flames then turn back to normal a few minutes later (HDHL1: Page 155)

VIII. DISTORTION OF VISION (NOT ACTUAL)

M. EVIDENCE OF INJURY, ILLNESS, OR BODY PROBLEM (ACTUALLY THERE)

I. BURNS/WELTS/SKIN IRRITATION

Sarah had a rash on the side of her face where something had brushed up against her (WDA: Page 157, 159)

After experiencing the feeling of being whipped, David had welts form on his back (DC: Page 146)

1. CROSS SHAPE

Maurice had burns in the shape of a cross on his palms (SH Loc 3315)

II. CUTS/SLASHING OF FLESH/STABBING

Roger awoke to his back, shoulders, rib cage clawed up (HDHL1: Page 187, 252, 255)

Mary found cuts on her arms (TH Loc 2004)

Carolyn was stabbed in her calf; a very deep wound caused by something invisible (HDHL1: Page 326); Carolyn was stabbed a separate time with a tomato stake in her hip; the stake wouldn't come out (HDHL2: Page 81)

Katie lifted her shirt to see a scratch on her stomach that burned; she also received scratches on her face multiple times (WDA: Page 34-35); a minute later Rachel had matching scratches on her face, neck, and arms (WDA: Page 35)

Aubrey was also attacked with scratches on her face and arms that bled (WDA: Page 35)

Both Brian and his older brother recall being scratched from time to time while living in the house (WDA: Page 69)

Eleonore began to be scratched by something; Harry saw them appear on her face randomly (WDA: Page 104)

The Cranmers had claw marks on them when they woke up (WDA: Page 95)

Maurice had stigmatic wounds on his feet (SH Loc 3321)

David was stabbed by the entities in the back and the side with their weapons from the spirit plane (DC: Page 105)

Debbie would wake up with scratches multiple times in the morning after being touched by a cold hand (DC: Page 216); Arne also woke up with strange scratches on his chest (DC: Page 216)

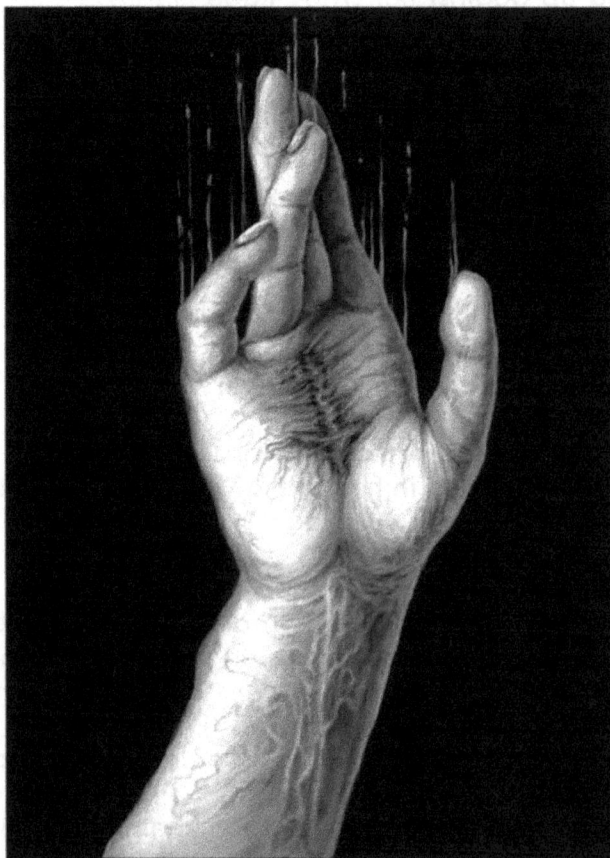

SHAPES / LETTERS

Maurice had a message carved into his back (SH Loc 1589, 2894)

Luciana had an N scratched into her stomach (BN: Page 28)

Luciana experienced a circle shape being scratched in her face (BN: Page 28)

A. PENTAGRAM

B. 666

Luciana had the number 666 written on her arm in welts (BN: Page 21)

III. BRUISING OR FINGER MARKS

Janet experienced visible bruising from multiple attacks (TH Loc 2694)

Nancy had finger marks on her neck where she had been choked (SH Loc 3179)

Cindy had bruises on her chin and elbows after being attacked by an entity (HDHL2: Page 73)

Doris would have bruises from the sexual attacks up and down her legs and on her inner thighs (WDA: Page 70)

The flying candelabras caused bruising on Doris' arm after they'd hit her (WDA: Page 76)

There were multiple times the Cranmers woke to bruising on their bodies (WDA: Page 95)

Janet's right arm had been gouged, which she discovered one morning when she woke up (TH Loc 2006)

David had visible finger marks on his neck after being choked by an invisible entity (DC: Page 87)

Jason came into the house limping because he had felt something kick him, which left bruises (DC: Page 95-96)

IV. BREAKING SKIN

Lesa had been pushed so hard into a wall that it broke the skin and bled (WDA: Page 98)

1. BITE MARKS

Jack had been bitten three times while he was showering (TH Loc 1626)

Janet had what looked like a bite on one of her fingers (TH Loc 2007)

Eleonore had been bitten visibly by the bullying entity (WDA: Page 103)

Hans witnessed bite marks appear up and down Eleonore's arms (WDA: Page 104)

Other people saw Clarita being bitten and blood coming to the surface of her skin from no known source (WDA: Page 106, 107)

2. PINPRICKS

Eleonore's skin would be pricked (WDA: Page 103); she also had a pinprick wound become infected repeatedly (WDA: Page 104)

V. SWELLING

Janet's finger swelled from a mysterious bite mark (TH Loc 2004)

Carolyn's calf swelled up strangely, more even than venom would have swelled it up (HDHLI: Page 327)

VI. BUMP/WOUND FROM ATTACK

Maurice had a nasty bump from the piece of wood hitting him on its own (SH Loc 2603)

VII. SLOW HEALING

It took days for Carolyn's mysterious calf muscle injury to heal (HDHLII Page 327)

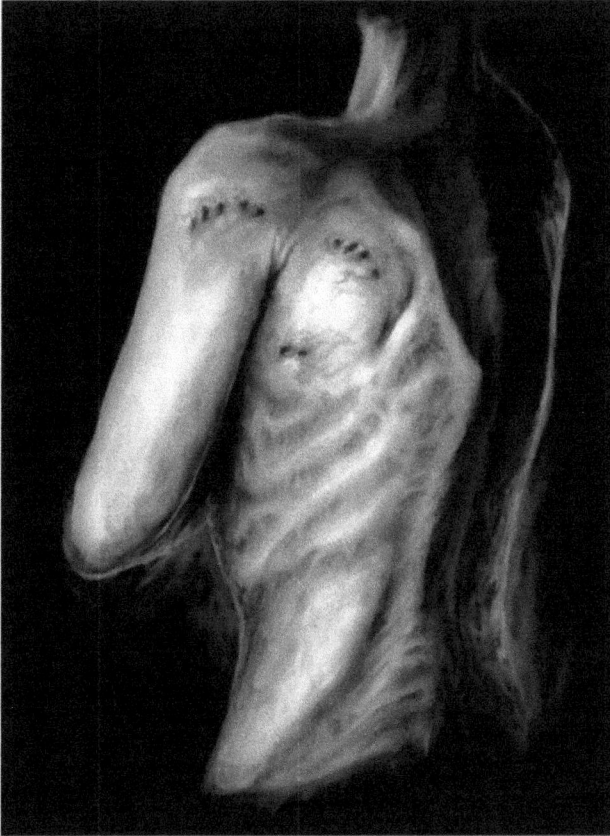

SOUND

Sound is interesting in demonic phenomena because of the way people convince themselves that there's no way they heard what they know they did[20]. I've had it happen myself where I'll be going to sleep and hear a voice speak to me; one time, I had one tell me, "Leave me alone." My response was obviously, "You leave me alone! What the hell!?" It's jarring even for people with psychic abilities such as myself; I can only imagine how scary it is for people not used to that sort of thing happening. The problem with classifying some of this activity is that human spirits were also in some of the narratives.

The intensity of phenomena informed which was which, though certain things like footsteps are one's guess; I included sections below with footsteps because they occurred in tandem with other known demonic phenomena. Common things that happen when dealing with demonic sounds are a voice that speaks aloud to the entire room or a familiar voice calling your name; there are also times that people hear inhuman voices in their heads along with malicious laughter121. Very heavy or loud footsteps and knocking are also heard, usually within the walls, often in threes—doors of all kinds are slammed122. Much of this sound phenomena is violent or unpleasant in some way for the hearer and happens without warning.

LEGEND

IDP = In a Dark Place
TH = The Haunted
SH = Satan's Harvest
HLHD1 = House of Light, House of Darkness, vol. 1
HLHD2= House of Light, House of Darkness, vol. 2
HLHD3 = House of Light, House of Darkness, vol. 3
BN = Beware the Night
WDA = When Demons Attack

SOUND

This section examines phenomena narrated by people who have heard (or should have been able to hear) something associated with the presence of an inhuman spirit.

N. VOICE DISTINCTION (OR NORMAL LACK THEREOF)

A voice spoke aloud from somewhere near a toy (BN: Page 54)

I. WHISPERINGS

Laura heard unintelligible whispering in the living room (IDP Loc 2934)
Michael also heard unintelligible whispering in his room (IDP Loc 3309)
Constant whispering was ongoing in the Smurl duplex (TH Loc 1657, 3650)
Janet heard whispering coming from closet (TH Loc 3130)

Kim and the dog, Simon, both turned in the bathroom when they heard whispering (TH Loc 3155)

An officer's audio recorder picked up a whispering voice overlaying it (WDA: Page 131)

When Arne went upstairs to investigate the stomping noise in the attic, he heard whisperings behind him (DC: Page 58)

Unintelligible whisperings were heard in the Glatzel home (DC: Page 96)

Alan heard unintelligible whisperings in the hallway after hearing a hissing noise in the master bedroom (DC: Page 142)

Carmen heard her name whispered quietly (IDP Loc 2526)

Carmen thought she heard whispered laughter but dismissed it as her imagination (IDP Loc 2526)

1. MULTIPLE WHISPERED VOICES AT ONCE

The Perron girls heard many voices whispering at night in their rooms (HDHLI: Page 206)

Jan heard multiple voices whispering to her when she knew she was alone (WDA: Page 83, 86)

II. CHANTING

Spirits surrounded Carolyn at one point in her bedroom, chanting ominously (HDHLI: Page 252)

Cindy heard chanting that got louder over time coming from inside the wall (HDHLI: Page 434, 457)

III. SILENT "BUBBLE" EFFECT

Carl and Alan got locked in the room with the waterbed and screamed for help but no one heart them (DC: Page 23)

When Cindy became trapped in an unlocked box, no one in her family could hear her screams; eventually, Nancy heard her whimper (HDHL2: Page 55)

An unnatural stillness would fall over the room when Tammy was awoken at night by the entity (DC: Page 46)

A deathly quiet fell over the space as the entity invaded

it with Ed watching (DC: Page 240)

1. PARTIAL "BUBBLE" EFFECT

Oddly, in the Glatzel home, some sounds would only be heard by a select few (DC: Page 63)

IV. VOCAL THREATS

David heard an apparition tell him out loud, "Beware!" in a threatening manner (DC: Page 33); David also heard a toy say the same thing to him when it appeared to come to life in front of him, adding that he would also be stabbed (DC: Page 99); Arne also heard this voice saying the same thing during his trial (DC: Page 292)

1. INHUMAN VOICE

A voice commanded a mother to stab her children (BN: Page 32)
The entity also threatened Katie, saying it would rape and kill her (WDA: Page 36)
An inhuman voice issued a command to Sarah aloud (WDA: Page 159)
David was told by the entity to take down a holy card of St. Michael along with all the crucifixes in the house or he would be punished (DC: Page 33)
David was threatened by the entity not to go to church (DC: Page 73)
David was consistently threatened of bodily harm by multiple entities (DC: Page 95)
Alan picked up the phone at one point and an inhuman voice told him he'd be stabbed (DC: Page 212)

A. SEXUAL

Ellie heard something tell her that it wanted to have sex with her in her ear (WDA: Page 33)

Sexual remarks were lobbed towards a mother while she was awake by something invisible (BN: Page 32)

The hairy beast issued sexual threats to Katie at night (WDA: Page 36); it also did this to Lisa (WDA: Page 39)

Monique heard in an ancient-sounding voice that the entity wanted to make love to her (BN: Page 91)

Kate received an obscene phone call where the entity told her what she was wearing and threatened to rape her; it also threatened her if she helped the Glatzels (DC: Page 212)

Vulgar phone calls reached several people in Brookfield one night unconnected to the Glatzels or their case (DC: Page 212)

2. FAMILIAR VOICE

A voice mimicking Carl Glatzel Sr. called the priests involved with David's case, threatening them to stay away; Carl Sr. hadn't called (DC: Page 212)

When Judy dialed her mother's number, her deceased husband answered the phone (WDA: Page 34)

V. LAUGHTER

Unspecified laughter heard by Stephen (IDP Loc 1064)
Voice laughs with Stephen audibly (IDP Loc 285)

1. INHUMAN/MALICIOUS

A voice laughed several times after saying horrible things to Carmen (IDP Loc 3568)

Al hears an evil chuckle in the basement (IDP Loc 3734)

Carmen hears evil laughter in the illusion (IDP Loc 4314)

Demonic laughter coming from Smurl duplex (TH Loc 3650)

Luciana heard inhuman laughter (BN: Page 29)

Katie heard the entity laugh after threatening her (WDA: Page 36)

Sarah heard inhuman laughter (WDA: Page 160)

2. MECHANICAL −SOUNDING

The beeping from the phone sounded like mechanized laughter (BN: Page 274)

VI. CALLING ONE'S NAME

Stephen hears his name called when no one in the house called for him (IDP Loc 583)

Stephen hearing his name called by unfamiliar voice (IDP Loc 525, 578)

Tammy had heard her name called by a voice that filled the room while living in the infested Newport house (DC: Page 46)

Stephen hears his name called several times in one sitting (IDP Loc 583-606, 848-853, 1499-1505, 2813, 2823)

Janet hears someone calling her name several times throughout the ordeal (TH Loc 386, 392, 397, 403, 409, 420)

Maurice heard his name called multiple times (SH Loc 2625)

David heard a terrible voice calling his name several times as he tried to sleep (DC: Page 65)

1. FAMILIAR VOICE

Stephen hears his father calling his name (IDP Loc 881)

Carmen hears Al calling her name (IDP Loc 965)

Janet's mother hears Jack calling her name (TH Loc 2719)

Mary heard her name called as well (TH Loc 2719)

Family voices were being imitated (TH Loc 3155)

The apparition of Gabby's father spoke to her several times (BN: Page 23)

DJ heard his grandfather's voice talking loudly in his ear several times (BN: Page 24)

Nancy's daughter heard her younger sister call her name, saw no one was there and then heard it again (BN: Page 227)

Christine heard her mother's voice telling her to get into a locked box where she wouldn't be able to breathe (HDHLI:

VII. MOANING /GROANING /SCREAMING

A neighbor and Dawn heard moaning in the campsite (TH Loc 3073)

Moaning happened while Janet was near (TH Loc 3124)

Moans and groans could be heard from the basement (BN: Page 27)

Kevin and Holly heard a woman moaning outside their window, which got louder and louder (WDA: Page 18, 26)

Henry heard screaming/wails that seemed to emanate from under the house (WDA: Page 141); Henry also heard screams coming up from under the earth where he'd found a Ouija board half-buried in the ground (WDA: Page 142)

Janet heard a man moaning sexually while she was in the tub (Th Loc 2359)

Al heard an inhuman-sounding groan in the basement (IDP Loc 3734)

Neighbors heard screams emitting from Smurl duplex (TH Loc 637)

Screams could be heard at night by the whole family (BN Page 26)

Holly and Kevin also heard a woman screaming outside their window (WDA: Page 18, 22, 26)

Doug heard crying coming from Lisa's room (WDA: Page 34)

VIII. MURMURING /UNINTELLIGIBLE VOICE

John heard a murmuring voice (IDP Loc 4575)

Maurice and Nancy heard a murmuring voice downstairs (SH Loc 1142)

Carmen heard angry murmuring (IDP Loc 2526)

IX. MANY VOICES /SOUNDS AT ONCE

Everyone in Snedeker household heard voices, multiple instances, unspecified language (IDP Loc 3655)

Many voices were heard in the kitchen (SH Loc 3278)

Snedeker house heard many voices speaking (IDP Loc 4780, 4786, 4792)

David heard muted screaming and squealing when the red light appeared in his room (DC: Page 66)

X. TALKING NORMALLY (PRESENCE IS SPEAKING)

1. TO A PERSON IN THE ROOM

Voices spoke aloud to each member of the family, often multiple times (IDP Loc 3713, 4635)

Stephen begins speaking to a voice that responds to him (IDP Loc 1829, 2461-2472, 2823-2835, 2946)

Shannon is spoken to by entity (Th Loc 2136)

The entity spoke to Gabby aloud (BN: Page 9, 16)

Eventually, the voice in Frank's head started to speak aloud (BN: 249)

Cindy heard a female voice telling her to come to them (HDHL2: Page 50)

A voice spoke aloud when addressed (WDA: Page 28)

The Countess heard a voice speak aloud in the room (WDA: Page 103) Henry was spoken to by the entity several times (WDA: Page 151)

A disembodied voice flirted with John (TH Loc 3150)

John heard an inhuman voice speaking to him (IDP Loc 4581, 4597-4614)

A. DISCARNATE (EMANATING FROM EVERYWHERE)

When the voice spoke in the Flynns' house, it didn't speak from one place but around the entire room (WDA: Page 28)

The voice that Tammy heard would fill the room in a very creepy way, calling her name (DC: Page 46)

A raspy, guttural voice threatened Snedekers that emanated from everywhere (IDP Loc 3433)

I. VOLUME INCREASING

While Cindy searched the room, the sound grew louder in intensity, enough to wake her siblings in nearby rooms (HDHLI: Page 347)

XI. IMITATING CHILDREN

1. LAUGHTER

Mary Smurl heard children laughing on other side of duplex (TH Loc 697)
The child on the phone would laugh at Erin (TH Loc 3522)

2. TANTRUM /CRYING

Sounds of a child throwing a tantrum came from upstairs (TH Loc 1905)
Judy's household often heard sounded of a crying baby (WDA: Page 34)

3. SOUNDS OF PLAYING /RUNNING

Mary Smurl also heard running around in an empty side of the duplex (TH Loc 697)

4. ANSWERING THE PHONE (NO CHILD IN HOUSE)

A child answered the phone when a friend called the Smurls (TH Loc 3522)

5. CALLING ONE'S NAME

Carmen heard her name called by a child's voice (IDP Loc 2526)

A young girl called David's name in the middle of the night several times, chilling him to the bone (DC: Page 141, 212)

6. IN AGONY

Ginny heard a baby crying as if it was frightened or in pain (BN: Page 228)

O. MISCELLANEOUS

I. HEARTBEAT (FILLS ROOM)

Jack heard a loud heartbeat sound (Th Loc 2799)

II. FOOTSTEPS /WALKING (NO PERSON PRESENT)

Carmen heard footsteps (IDP Loc 1438, 1443)

Laura heard footsteps (IDP Loc 2922)

Chris, a researcher helping with the case, heard footsteps (IDP Loc 4565)

Jack heard footsteps upstairs (TH Loc 363)

Heavy footsteps in the attics were heard by the Smurls (TH Loc 860)

Maurice and Nancy heard walking around at night (SH Loc 1703)

Nancy heard footsteps in her closet, on the stairs when no one was there (HDHL1: Page 208) Roger heard footsteps coming up the cellar stairs (HDHL1: Page 450)/ (HDHL2: Page 192)

Judy and her family often heard footsteps right before phenomena started up (WDA: Page 34, 37)

Sarah heard footsteps in her room that sounded like boots (WDA: Page 156); others heard creaking floorboards in the house (WDA: Page 157)

Tammy consistently heard footsteps up in the attic while living in an infested house (DC: Page 46)

When Kate had stored some of the Glatzel's things in her basement, she swore she'd started to hear someone down there (DC: Page 84)

1. SHUFFLING FEET

Stephen heard shuffling feet (IDP Loc 853)

2. FROM OUTSIDE

Laura heard footsteps outside the house (IDP Loc 2934)
Angelo heard heavy footsteps, like a man was walking outside (BN: Page 64,65)

3. RUNNING SOUNDS

Angelo heard something running back and forth over his head (BN: Page 65)

4. UNNATURALLY LOUD /BOOMING

The footsteps that issued from the Glatzel's attic boomed loudly then the same sound was suddenly happening in the kitchen DC: Page 58)
Jen heard heavy footsteps coming up from the basement (BN: Page 66)
Ginny heard loud footsteps walking upstairs above her (BN: Page 228)
Very, very loud footsteps could be heard throughout the house (WDA: Page 94)
Everyone in the house heard footsteps from the basement (WDA: Page 123)
Nancy heard very loud footsteps upstairs while home alone (HDHLI: Page 459)
Holly and Kevin heard heavy footsteps walking down their staircase coming towards them (WDA: Page 18)
The Glatzels heard many, many footsteps walking loudly above them in the attic (DC: Page 77)
A stomping sound was heard shortly after the rocking chair was seemingly occupied (DC: Page 156)

III. HEAVY BREATHING

Maurice heard heavy breathing several times (SH Loc 1703)

Judy heard breathing in her ear, which woke her up (WDA: Page 33)

Tammy would either hear her name or heavy breathing filling a room when she was awoken at night (DC: Page 46)

IV. WHISTLE / WHISTLING

Janet heard lascivious whistling while she was in the bathtub (TH Loc 1357)

Barbara heard a deafening whistle out of nowhere (WDA: Page 37)

V. SLAPPING / HITTING SOUND

Jack and Janet heard a slap sound when she was hit (TH Loc 1259)

When David was shoved backward by an invisible force, a noticeable thud was hurt as he was hit (DC: Page 68)

VI. HUMMING / VIBRATION

The barn would hum while the girls would play in the barn's hayloft (HDHL1: Page 211)

David heard a strange humming vibration start up in his room when he witnessed the red light (DC: Page 66); this same phenomena preceding the red orb sighting was experienced by the rest of the family (DC: Page 158)

Strange humming vibrations plagued the Glatzels several times throughout their orderal (DC: Page 80, 144, 213)

VII. RECORDING ISSUES (NOTHING RECORDED)

The tapes didn't pick up any supernatural event when the people there heard them (SH Loc 3150)

When Alan tried to record the humming sound, David accurately pointed out that this wouldn't work (DC: Page 144)

VIII. GUNSHOT SOUND (FROM APPORT)

Ralph heard a gunshot as his medal appeared out of nowhere, having been moved by a demonic entity from one place to another (BN: Page 55)

IX. GALE FORCE WINDS (HEARD)

The Glatzels heard a gale force wind blowing outside but when Debbie checked out the window, it was perfectly still (DC: Page 76)

The wind outside Kate's house was so loud that it got her out of bed to check what was happening (DC: Page 84)

X. EXPLOSION SOUND

A sound like an explosion from David and Alan's room awoke all of the Glazels in the middle of the night (DC: Page 144)

XI. MUSIC

Al was awakened by several sounds and one of them was the sound of vintage music playing downstairs when all should have been quiet (IDP: Page 119)

P. ANIMAL MIMICRY /SOUNDS (NONE PRESENT)

I. ROARING /HOWLING /GROWLING / SNORTING /SCREECHING

Nancy heard an animal howling (SH Loc 2491)

Cindy heard something growling in her room (HDHL1: Page 347) / (HDHL2: Page 49)

The sound of a growling animal would often be heard in Judy's house (WDA: Page 34)

Barbara heard roaring in her ears (WDA: Page 37)

A horrible growling was heard the second Father Sheehan took a step towards the Glatzel's door (DC: Page 163)

Cindy and Katy were tormented by roars that they could hear even as they covered their ears (HDHL2: Page 36)

There was an imitation of a cat sound when there wasn't one (TH Loc 3160)

A dog was heard growling though the Ammons nor their neighbors had a dog (WDA: Page 123-124)

The tapes picked up pigs squealing in the background of the Smurl house (TH Loc 1825)

Tammy heard the sounds of chickens at night (and only at night) but there were none nor had there ever been chickens on the premises since she lived there (DC: Page 46)

The Smurl children heard hissing like invisible snakes (TH Loc 860) 47

Mary heard hissing on her side of the duplex (TH Loc 1938)

Alan heard hissing as if from a large snake emitting from the master bedroom (DC: Page 142)

Janet heard the hybrid creature snort, a horrible sound that made her feel nauseous (TH Loc 2815)

Ed heard screeching sounds in the distance when this entity appeared to him (DC: Page 240)

1. FLUTTERING /RUSTLING SOUND (GIGANTIC WINGS)

A neighbor heard fluttering sound from upstairs window (TH Loc 637, 2917)

Carin had heard a fluttering sound in her room (TH Loc 820)

The Smurl children heard fluttering of wings in the chimney (TH Loc 825)

Kevin heard the rustling sound of huge wings in the room with him (WDA: Page 28)

2. HOOVES

Chris heard the sound of animal hooves on the walls and ceiling (TH Loc 1808)

Jack heard hooves as the hybrid chased after him (TH Loc 2821)

Jack heard hooves on the camper roof (TH Loc 3046)

The Smurls kept hearing the hooves on the camper roof (TH Loc 3068)

3. TORTURED ANIMAL SOUNDS

Gabby heard tormented animal sounds (BN: Page 9)

A. INABILITY TO BREATHE

Simon, the family dog, was gasping and unable to breathe well (TH Loc 2794)

4. EATING SOUNDS

Nancy had heard what sounded like an animal eating (SH Loc 2491)

A. SLOBBERING SOUND

Jack heard a creature make a slobbering sound (TH Loc

Q. LOUD OBJECT-RELATED SOUNDS

A crashing sound came from the dresser Diane was standing near (TH Loc 1165)

A crash rang out from somewhere in the house (WDA: Page 29)

Unspecified movement was heard upstairs while the Glatzel family attempted to sleep (DC: Page 70)

Overhead, the Glatzels heard something loudly being dropped in the attic when no one was up there (DC: Page 77)

Guy and Frankie heard a cannonball rolling across the floor (HDHL2: Page 246)

I. KNOCKINGS /POUNDINGS /BANGING /TAPPING

The cellar door would be consistently pounded on in the Perron home (HDHL1: Page 301)

Carolyn's door was pounded on so loudly that she felt it in her ribcage (HDHL1: Page 307) Loud poundings would erupt randomly from the walls and floors (WDA: Page 94)

Rapping were heard on the walls of Eleonore's room (WDA: Page 103)

Knocking was often heard on the front door of the Ammon residence (WDA: Page 124)

A delicate kind of tapping started issuing from the living room window (DC: Page 58)

Everyone in the Glatzel family was awoken at precisely three in the morning by pounding on the house (DC: Page 60)

At one point, the pounding was so intense on Judy and Carl's window that it seemed like the glass would break but it didn't (DC: Page 61)

Something pounded on the door to the Perron house one night (HDHL1: Page 307)

Kevin and Holly would settle into bed then heard loud knocking that would intensify as they went to answer the door (WDA: Page 17, 18, 22, 26)

Knockings, pounding, and rappings were consistently heard throughout the Glatzel's ordeal (DC: Page 66, 86, 96)

Knocks on doors, taps on windows were common for Megan and Jennifer to experience in the Newport house (DC: Page 141)

Carl Sr. felt something hit the floor of the house from underneath (DC: Page 172)

1. IN THREES (TRINITY KNOCKS)

Pounding on house happens three times (IDP Loc 3184)

Smurls heard knocks in threes (TH Loc 1272, 2723)

Dawn heard three knocks on the door (TH Loc 2789)

Nancy heard knocks happening outside in patterns of three (SH Loc 2586)

Pounding in three was happening on her night table (BN: Page 91)

Roger heard three loud knocks at the door (HDHLI: Page 309)

Everyone in the house at the time of David's prophecy about the spirit being on its way heard the three knocks (DC: Page 46); three more knocks issued on front door later that night (DC: Page 57)

Three knocks resounded at the front door followed by rapping on the outside of the house (DC: Page 95)

Three thumps hit the floor while Ed and Lorraine were in the Glatzel house (DC: Page 121)

Three knocks were heard directly after the stomping phenomena then again soon after (DC: Page 156-157)

Three knocks were heard on the front door; when answered, it revealed that nobody was there (DC: Page 162)

A. SWITCHING FROM FRONT TO BACK DOOR INSTANTANEOUSLY

Kevin would investigate one door being knocked on only to have the other one knocked on/vice versa (WDA: Page 17)

2. FROM WITHIN WALLS OR FROM FLOORS
(NON-THREES)

The family heard the pounding coming from inside the walls (IDP Loc 3410)

Snedeker family (and relatives) hear a sound reverberate through the house (IDP Loc 3178, 3438)

Pounding happened within the Smurl duplex's walls many times (TH Loc 744, 1253, 2322, 3393, 3543, 3650)

Knocks came from within the Smurl's walls (TH Loc 1247, 1328, 2673, 3124)

Ricky and Brad heard knocking in the Smurl house (TH Loc 1419, 1435)

Chris hears pounding in walls (TH Loc 1808)

Mary hears tapping in the walls (TH Loc 1938)

Dawn hears banging inside the walls of the bathroom (TH Loc 1989)

Neighbor hears tapping coming from Smurls' windows (Th Loc 2917)

Once the entity disappeared, Bob's family would hear it moving around inside the walls (WDA: Page 95)

Four knocks sounded like they came from the floor in the Glatzel home (DC: Page 78-79)

A huge pounding came from the floor while Ed and Lorraine were there (DC: Page 121)

3. ON/WITHIN FURNITURE

Rapping noises emitted from within furniture (Th Loc 2195)

Pounding happened from within the closet (TH Loc 2794)

Knocking and banging happened in Theriault household (SH Loc 1703, 3273, 3302)

Ellie heard knocks coming from her nightstand, continually repeating (WDA: Page 33)

Rapping noises emitted from within furniture (TH Loc 2195)

Knockings from the Glatzel's table began (DC: Page 86, 121)

4. ON VEHICLES

The entity rapped hard and loudly on the floor and roof of the camper (TH: Page 182)

5. WITHIN RADIO

The radio in Jack's office began to tap from within (Th Loc 2167)

6. TAPPING /RATTLING

Investigators heard doorknobs rattling in empty rooms (BN: Page 30)

7. TV

The TV turned on full volume at night (BN: Page 27)

II. SLAMMING OF DOORS /WINDOWS

Carmen heard doors slamming in the house (IDP Loc 1443)
Laura had the door slam on her when she tried to leave the bathroom (IDP Loc 3399)
Doors slammed in Smurl duplex occasionally (TH Loc 571, 900)
Cupboard doors slammed in Smurl's kitchen (TH Loc 1905)
Doors would be slammed randomly (BN: Page 36)
The closet door opened suddenly and slammed against the wall hard enough to leave a dent (BN: Page 75)
Carmen heard doors slamming in the house (IDP Loc 1443)

III. SCRATCHING (NON-ANIMAL)

Ralph heard scratching noises in the corner of a room (BN: Page 175)

1. WITHIN WALLS /CEILING

The Smurl children heard scratching in the walls like claws (TH Loc 814)

Angelo was woken up by scratching noises in the ceiling (BN: Page 63, 64)

Henry heard scratching/clawing noises coming from the walls/ceilings (WDA: Page 148)

The kids heard what sounded like mice scratching in the walls; none were found when checked (WDA: Page 157)

The Glatzels heard what sounded like scratching coming from inside the walls several times in the same sitting (DC: Page 58)

While David was being attacked, scratching sounds started up in the walls (DC: Page 69)

2. WITHIN FURNITURE

Chris heard scratching in Mary's hutch (TH Loc 1813)

3. ON GLASS

Lorraine heard scratching on the glass (TH Loc 1511)

IV. SWIRLING /SWISHING /RUSHING /RUSTLING SOUND

A rustling sound could be heard from within drawers (TH Loc 1165)

A swishing sound was heard from Kevin's nephew's room (WDA: Page 126)

Something could be heard roving around the room quickly to reach Sarah (WDA: Page 159)

1. CHAIR ROCKING SOUND

Jack and Janet heard lawn chairs on porch rocking (TH Loc 363)

V. OPENING AND /OR CLOSING

1. DRAWERS

Jack heard drawers opening and closing upstairs (TH Loc 363)

2. DOORS

Holly heard the door open behind her when no one was there (WDA: Page 15)
Holly and Kevin both heard their front door creak open then during the same experience, their son's door (WDA: Page 17, 22)
Aubrey and Ellie watched as their door was flung open by itself (WDA: Page 38)
The basement door would creak open several times (WDA: Page 123)

VI. RATTLING /SHAKING

Drawers began to shake of a dresser (TH Loc 1165)
Doorknob began to vibrate (BN: Page 16)
The bunk shook violently while two girls were on it (BN: Page 21)
Jen heard the door rattling like a break-in (BN: Page 245)
Kevin and Holly heard a rumbling, movement sound (WDA: Page 13, 24, 28)

R. AUDITORY ILLUSIONS

I. INHUMAN VOICE IN MIND (UNHEARD BY OTHERS)

Laura heard awful things in her mind being said to her (IDP Loc 4517)
Carmen heard inhuman voices speak to her, say frightening things (IDP Loc 4231-4268, 4290)

Al heard the voice from the horrific Christ illusion speak to him aloud (IDP Loc 4173)

Al heard a voice speak to him in his head (IDP Loc 4710), then returned to yell at him during the exorcism (IDP Loc 4746)

Jessica heard a statue talk to her (SH Loc 3086)

Frank heard a voice speaking inside his own head (BN: Page 248)

The hairy beast spoke to Katie in her mind (WDA: Page 36)

The granddaughter heard a voice that told her that she'd never see her family again because she'd be dead in twenty minutes (WDA: Page 125)

David was often spoken to and threatened by the spirit that he'd come across in the Newport house, a voice unheard by anyone else; this voice also threatened others through David (DC: Page 33-37, 43, 50-51, 57, 61-63, 69-70, 73, 75, 77-79, 81, 86, 95, 99, 105, 107-108, 133, 144-145, 196, 231, 255, 266)

When these entities would have meetings in the Glatzel's kitchen, they would sometimes speak in languages David couldn't identify or understand; they also often chanted (DC: Page 166)

Jennifer received a message from the entity only meant for her to hear about Arne's fate (DC: Page 265)

Jason heard the entity say terrible things to him about death and destruction (DC: Page 297)

Henry claimed to hear the entity laugh at the Reverend that only he could hear in his head (WDA: Page 151)

Yves heard a jeering laugh that echoed and a faint wailing that no one else could hear (HD: Page 117)

1. CHANTING (UNHEARD BY OTHERS)

The entities tormenting David began to chant together, which only David could likely hear and an orb appeared (DC: Page 100)

II. YELLING (UNHEARD BY OTHERS)

Jack's parents heard yelling and profanity emanating

from Jack and Janet's side of the duplex (TH Loc 431)

III. CAR SOUNDS (NOT ACTUAL)

A car heard slamming outside with no one there (SH Loc 2924, 3302)
A car heard approaching (SH Loc 3007, 3075)
A horn kept being heard by Andrea that would increase in volume and get more disturbing as time went on (HDHL1: Page 457)
A horn sounded in the house, heard by everyone (HDHL2: Page 172, 196. 197)

IV. SCRATCHING SOUNDS (NOT ACTUAL)

Jessica heard scratching sounds under the couch (SH Loc 3070)

V. RADIOS ON (NONE THERE)

A radio was heard that wasn't there (SH Loc 3080)

VI. DRAGGING FURNITURE SOUNDS (NOT ACTUAL)

Nancy (and others with her during a party) distinctly heard furniture being dragged across the floor upstairs but nothing was moved (HDHL1: Page 461, 463, 464)

VII. INANIMATE OBJECT APPEARING TO SPEAK

David experienced a toy coming to life in front of him in the middle of the night then speaking to him (DC: Page 99)

S. ELECTRICAL/APPLIANCE PROBLEMS (HEARD)

I. TOILETS FLUSHING

The Smurls heard toilets flushing by themselves several

times (TH Loc 363)

II. FAUCETS TURNING ON AND /OR OFF

Mary heard the faucets turning on and off (TH Loc 2014)
The kitchen faucet turned on by an invisible hand (BN: Page 269)
Faucets began to turn on and off on their own (WDA: Page 157)

III. HEARD PHONE PHENOMENA

1. STRANGE RINGING OF PHONE /ACCOMPANYING PHONE

The phone in Jack's office started to ring strangely (TH Loc 2157)
The fire alarm sound started going off when the phone rang (TH Loc 2157)
The phone in Jack's office started to ring strangely (TH Loc 2157)

IV. LIGHTS TURNING ON AND /OR OFF (HEARD)

Carmen heard the lights flick off (IDP Loc 1443)

V. STATIC /BEEPING

Mike kept having his conversation interrupted by static then eventually disconnected (BN: Page 261)
Donna kept having incessant beeping on her phone (BN: Page 263)
An entity began to communicate through beeps on a phone line, answering questions to Mike and Donna (BN: Page 263)

VI. RADIO ISSUES

A radio that had been dead for years would play at deafening levels or play white noise (HDHL3: Page 72)

In a police car, the radio had static, and voice came through (WDA: Page 132)

A radio in Bob and Lesa's house would turn on by itself (WDA: Page 94)

SMELL

This section covers the narratives of people who have experienced strange smells associated with demonic presences.

LEGEND

IDP = In a Dark Place
TH = The Haunted
SH = Satan's Harvest
HLHD1 = House of Light, House of Darkness, vol. 1
HLHD2= House of Light, House of Darkness, vol. 2
HLHD3 = House of Light, House of Darkness, vol. 3
BN = Beware the Night
WDA = When Demons Attack

T. BODILY FLUIDS OR ODORS

I. BLOOD

The smell of blood filled Carmen's kitchen while she

mopped the floor (IDP Loc 1007, 2703)

II. FECES /RAW SEWAGE

The Smurls smelled feces, which filled the entire house upon their arrival (TH Page 186)
Investigators smell feces in the Theriault house (SH Loc 2631)
The Snedekers would smell feces in the house that dissipated quickly even though it was such an intense smell (IDP Page 264); this smell would often make the Snedekers' eyes water (IDP Loc 3719)
Al gagged on the overpowering excrement smell (IDP Loc 3751)
Mary smelled raw sewage on her side of the duplex (TH Loc 1938)
Al had tears in his eyes from the raw sewage smell that appeared in the house (IDP Page 266)

III. BREATH (FROM ENTITY)

Cindy could smell the hot breath of this entity, terrifying her further (HDHL1: Page 349)
Ellie smelled the terrible smell of an entity's breath near her head (WDA: Page 33)

IV. SEMEN

V. URINE

VI. VOMIT

U. RANCID /DECOMPOSITION SCENTS

Katy and Cindy smelled something rancid in the room with them (HDHL2: Page 35); Katy gagged from the stench (HDHL2: Page 35)
Rotting smells often permeated the Snedeker residence (IDP Loc 4635)

Jack smelled something fetid in the room (TH Loc 2799); Janet noticed the same smell when she awoke a few minutes later (TH Loc 2832)

David also smelled an acrid, rotting odor when he came into Jonathan's room (HD: Page 167)

I. ROTTING FOOD

Nancy smelled rotting potatoes in her kitchen (SH Page 141)

Rotten eggs were smelled by team (BN: Page 28)

The Snedekers at one point smelled rotting meat (IDP Loc 3713); Al smelled this scent in the basement (IDP Loc 3746); this particular smell was eye-watering (IDP Loc 3746) and induced gagging in Al (IDP Loc 3746)

The rotting potatoes smell would disappear as Nancy tried to locate the source (SH Page 141)

II. ROTTING GARBAGE

Jack and Janet smelled rotting garbage in their room (TH Loc 749)

Janet smelled rotting garbage in their car (TH Loc 2014)

Carmen and Laura detected a smell of garbage that filled up the room (IDP Loc 3821)

The garbage smell in Janet and Jack's room made them gag and have to leave the room (TH Loc 744)

III. ROTTING FLESH

The scent of rotting flesh emitted from horde of flawed apparitions (IDP Loc 4780)

The boys smelled something that reminded them of rotting flesh as they walked into their mother's room (WDA: Page 71, 75)

Sarah smelled rotting flesh in her room several times (WDA: Page 156, 157, 159)

Sarah and Justin experienced the house fill up with such a revolting smell that they both vomited (WDA: Page 162)

The smell of rotting flesh from the flawed apparitions disappeared as soon as the entities did (IDP Page 338)

The decay of rotting flesh hit Ed as soon as the demon entered the room (DC: Page 240)

IV. ODOR COMBINATIONS

A terrible mixture of burning rubber and sulfur would accompany the entity manifesting (WDA: Page 94)

Jan smelled a combination of decaying eggs and flesh in her basement so strong it made her gag and retch (WDA: Page 85)

V. OTHER (MISCELLANEOUS)

I. ODD, DISTINCT SMELLS (NOT UNPLEASANT)

The creature Janet saw had a smell that wasn't offensive (TH Loc 503)

II. OTHER FOUL SMELLS (UNSPECIFIED)

A horrible stench filled Ed's nose during an experience with the entity (TH Loc 1573)

Chris smelled something horrible while he was calling upon divine assistance (TH Loc 1818)

Mary's bedroom had a terrible smell (TH Loc 2014)

Foul smells would issue in the camper while the Smurls tried to relax (TH Page 185)

Shannon smelled something bad when she'd seen a flawed apparition (TH Loc 3185)

A reporter smelled a foul odor when in the Smurl house (TH Loc 3352)

Foul smells happened periodically in the Theriault house (SH Loc 1703)

Robert had a foul smell fill his car (SH Loc 2476)

Carolyn smelled something terrible around her (HDHLI:

Page 423)

A horrific smell filled the room that Cindy and Lori were in, making them gag (HDHL2: Page 24)

Frankie smelled something terrible filling up the room that nearly caused retching (HDHL2: Page 246)

Disgusting smells would fill up entire rooms in Jan and Brandon's home (WDA: Page 86)

The Cranmer house had a terrible stench permeate the entire space (WDA: Page 98)

Ed and Lorraine smelled several foul things in the Snedeker house (IDP Loc 4376)

John smelled something rotten when confronted with the hybrid entity (IDP Loc 4586)

III. CELLAR / MILDEW

Jack's office began to smell like an old cellar when it hadn't before (Th Loc 2162)

Jerry almost threw up from the death smell in his car (HDHL1: Page 466)

IV. DEATH

There was a smell of death that returned many times in the house (HDHL1: Page 118, 128, 131, 134, 137-138, 149, 155, 187, 228)/ (HDHL2: Page 174, 191)

Cindy had continual experiences with an entity that smelled like death (HDHL1: Page 206, 210, 222)/ (HDHL2: Page 50, 253)/ (HDHL3: Page 169)

Nancy had experiences with the death odor that accompanied a spirit in the room with her (HDHL1: Page 208, 212)

Cathi had a death smell erupt in her car (HDHL1: Page 235)

Carolyn smelled the familiar death stench as many entities surrounded her (HDHL1: Page 251)

Jerry smelled a death-like odor in his car (HDHL1: Page 466)

Roger continually smelled death each time the entity approached him (HDHL2: Page 123, 125)

Carolyn's stomach retched from the death smell (HDHL 1: Page 187, 253)

V. WOODSMOKE /BURNING

Jack smelled wood-burning (TH Loc 3290, 3295)
Justin and Sarah woke up to the smell of something burnt (WDA: Page 157)

VI. GREASE

Down in the funeral home prep rooms (basement) was a lingering greasy smell (IDP Loc 438)

VII. PERFUME OR COLOGNE (OVERPOWERING)

Jill smelled a man's cologne, distinct from her husband that was overpowering (BN: Page 75)
Ralph smelled overpowering sweet perfume in a bedroom (BN: Page 87)

FEELING

Something I've noticed about demonic narratives is the unwillingness to listen to what one's body is saying. Especially in cases of Already Inhabited, where a demon is currently living in the home one has bought or rented, everyone immediately realizes that something's wrong127. They can feel it; this is our evolutionary brain at work, trying to keep us safe from the threat that we sense. More psychically inclined people tend to notice the presence with them much quicker and in a more detailed way, but even people who are about as psychic as mud sense something on a primal level. They tell themselves to shake it off, to stop being silly, that it's just an old house or apartment and they're always a little creepy. It's only when sight comes into play that people begin to reevaluate since seeing is believing and all their feelings are taken into account128.

Common phenomena from the Feeling section includes being grabbed/yanked on, having your body pushed or held down by an invisible force, and odd vibrations129. Freezing temperatures are incredibly common, as is the feeling that you're not alone with something malicious/unseen, feeling immobilized, scratched or bitten, along with newly formed anger issues usually paired with depression. It is important to take care of your mental health if you feel it is suffering. Address that first before anything else when it comes to the supernatural because it will become a problem eventually.

CLASS 4: FEELING
This section encompasses the feelings associated with an inhuman encounter.

LEGEND

IDP = In a Dark Place
TH = The Haunted
SH = Satan's Harvest
HLHD1 = House of Light, House of Darkness, vol. 1
HLHD2= House of Light, House of Darkness, vol. 2
HLHD3 = House of Light, House of Darkness, vol. 3
BN = Beware the Night
WDA = When Demons Attack

FEELING (OR EXPERIENCED)

W. VIOLENT FELT MOVEMENT

The Snedekers continually felt violent attacks on their bodies day and night (IDP Loc 4635)

I. SHOVING/HURLED/THROWN

Carmen was shoved on the bed in front of Laura (IDP Loc 3831)
Carmen was shoved on the porch steps by something invisible (IDP Loc 4214)
Al was shoved onto the bed by extremely strong but invisible hands (IDP Loc 4349)
Ed was shoved down on the bed by an invisible presence (TH Page 91)
The Smurls' dog was picked up and thrown by invisible hands into the kitchen door (TH Page 50)

Shannon was thrown down the stairs while everyone was in bed (TH Page 52)

Shannon was thrown out of bed and onto the floor violently (TH Page 123)

Maurice was suddenly picked up and thrown like he was a doll (SH Page 26)

Luciana was thrown to the ground several times by the entity, often without warning (BN: Page 25)

Doris' oldest son watched helplessly as she was thrown around the room (WDA: Page 70)

Jason was shoved off the top bunk by something invisible and hit his head on the ground (DC: Page 107)

Arne was picked up by something invisible and thrown off the porch steps one day (DC: Page 115)

1. HELD DOWN /AGAINST WALL /PUSHING OR PRESSING DOWN

Carmen was shoved then held against the shower wall by an entity saying obscene things to her (IDP Page 254)

Carmen felt several hands pressing her down before she was sexually violated by the entity (IDP Page 252)

During sexual attacks, many people feel heavy pressure on their limbs and chest (BN: Page 30)

Nancy felt crushed by an invisible force (HDHL1: Page 212)

Aubrey felt something push down on her chest (WDA: Page 38)

The hairy entity crawled on top of Lisa while the blanket was over her head (WDA: Page 39)

Katie felt she was being smothered as the shadow figure's mass covered her on the mattress (WDA: Page 40); Ellie also had this happen (WDA: Page 40) and so did Aubrey eventually (WDA: Page 41)

Henry was held down by an invisible presence so he couldn't get away (WDA: Page 141)

Sarah felt weight descend on her body during multiple nights (WDA: Page 156, 157, 159)

One night, the weight became unbearable as if Sarah

were being crushed (WDA: Page 159)

David's head was pushed down while he was in Mass by an unseen force (DC: Page 74)

2. NECK GRABBED /CHOKING

Ed felt something choking him as he began a prayer out loud (TH Page 90)

The disembodied hand in the mattress grabbed Janet's neck and held it (TH Page 187)

Nancy was choked by invisible force (SH Loc 3167)

Rosa felt something choke her when she went into the basement (WDA: Page 125)

Sarah was choked one night so hard that it felt like her neck would snap (WDA: Page 159)

David felt himself being choked by an invisible entity (DC: Page 87, 146, 157)

Aubrey couldn't breathe when the entity knelt on her chest while she was awake (WDA: Page 38)

II. HAVING A BODY PART OR CLOTHING MOVED/YANKED/ GRABBED /BEING DRAGGED

Tendrils of smoke that formed claws grabbed at the Snedekers (IDP Page 337)

Gabby was yanked to graveyard/specific headstone (BN: Page 14)

Luciana felt her hair being yanked on several times (BN: Page 25, 33)

Lori and Cindy felt their hair being pulled by something invisible (HDHL2: Page 23); on a separate occasion, Cindy felt her hair yanked to the ground (HDHL2: Page 253)

Cindy had her legs being pulled on something as she held onto her doorways (HDHL2: Page 71)

Both of Doris' sons felt their body parts pulled on at some point in time (WDA: Page 69)

The entity would pull Eleonore's hair (WDA: Page 103)

Judy's hair was yanked during the night by an unseen force (DC: Page 70)

Arne felt his wrist grabbed by an ice-cold hand (DC: Page 70)

Dawn felt her arms grabbed and twisted behind her (TH Loc 1989)

Brady had his shoulders yanked one way then the other (TH Loc 1620)

Laura felt an invisible hand tug on her bra (IDP Page 241)

Janet was dragged out of her bed and onto the floor (TH Loc 733)

Cindy felt her bed moved from one end of the room to the other every night (HDHL1: Page 431)

Judy felt her hair pulled by something invisible (DC: Page 96)

Jason felt a hand yank his ankle down that made him trip (DC: Page 107)

Arne felt something ice cold grab his ankle and trip him (DC: Page 141)

David began to be yanked up by his shirt by the entity until Arne threw holy water in that direction (DC: Page 157)

III. SEXUAL-RELATED ATTACKS AND /OR TOUCHING (WHILE AWAKE)

Laura felt fingers between her legs that entered her while alone (IDP Loc 3289, 3805)

Laura felt something slide up her thigh while in the bathroom, trying to penetrate her (IDP Loc 3393)

Carmen felt a hand slide up her thighs and press upward (IDP Loc 3528, 3540)

Chris, a researcher, felt like he was groped in his crotch (IDP Loc 4527) then fondled (IDP Loc 4532)

Janet was touched by something sexually until prayer and holy water pushed it back (TH Page 150)

Dawn felt something brush past her, an invisible entity but imitating the way a man might (TH Page 115)

Debbie felt her thigh being rubbed during the night (DC:

Page 70)

Luciana had her legs forced apart by something invisible (BN: Page 29)

Laura feels something touching her legs a few times in one sitting (IDP Loc 3284)

A friend of a researcher had his pants unbuckled that then slid down by themselves (SH Loc 3065)

Judy felt a hard pinch on her butt by an invisible entity (DC: Page 85)

Laura felt her breasts be pinched painfully (IDP Loc 3399, 3836); Carmen also had this exact same thing happen to her (IDP Loc 3568)

Chris felt his penis be squeezed by a spirit (IDP Page 320)

Debbie felt something invisible stroke her thigh suggestively (DC: Page 83)

1. VAGINAL RAPE

Carmen felt something enter her (IDP Loc 3540)

Carmen was raped in the bathroom by an invisible force (IDP Loc 3568)

Laura felt something thrusting itself between her legs (IDP Loc 3842)

Maurice's stepdaughter had been raped by Maurice's doppelganger several times (SH Loc 3476)

Ellie was raped by the shadow figure (WDA: Page 40)

Judy was also raped, but by the hairy creature (WDA: Page 41)

Doris was raped by the entity in her home (WDA: Page 69)

Sarah was sexually assaulted by the entity during several nights (WDA: Page 156, 157, 159)

2. RECTAL RAPE

Carmen was rectally raped by an unseen force (IDP Loc 3546)

Al was rectally raped (IDP Loc 4355)

Carl felt something enter him rectally (BN: Page 29)

Jessica was rectally raped by the entity (BN: Page 113)
Aubrey was rectally raped by the entity in her room (WDA: Page 41)

IV. TWISTED AROUND /SPUN/SIDE TO SIDE MOVEMENT

Maurice felt the ladder he was on twisted from side to side (SH Loc 1733)

1. BUMPING INTO WALL /BOUNCING AGAINST WALL (MIDAIR)

Maurice felt himself bounce off the walls (SH Loc 2744)

2. TWISTED AROUND FROM MIDAIR

Maurice was twisted around while already in midair (SH Loc 2744)
The bed was levitated in camper was jerked around mid-air (Th Loc 3007)

V. OBJECT–RELATED VIOLENT FELT MOVEMENT

1. OBJECTS YANKED AWAY (FELT)

A rosary was yanked away from Laura (IDP Loc 3799)
Carmen had a rosary yanked from her hands then broke (IDP Page 274)
Maurice had a rosary yanked out of his hand (SH Loc 2288)
Religious jewelry would be yanked from people's bodies in the Cranmer home (WDA: Page 96)
Maurice had the steering wheel yanked out of his hand while driving (SH Loc 1523)
Janet felt her blanket being tugged off her (TH Loc 2678)
Maurice had a ladder yanked forcibly from under him (SH Loc 1739, 1748)

2. OBJECT ATTACKING PERSON

A piece of wood hit Maurice held by an invisible force (SH Loc 2603)

Ralph's St. Benedict medal hit him in the neck after the object was apported (BN: Page 55)

Carolyn had a hanger attack her neck and shoulders of its own accord (HLHD1: Page 105)

Doris felt the poster boards fall from the ceiling on top of her head (WDA: Page 76)

Eleanore felt small things in her house begin to pelt down on her (WDA: Page 102)

A makeup case levitated off a table and hit David square in the chest; when it was returned to its place, the case hit his ear and then again, a third time (DC: Page 143)

David's scapulars would be wrapped around his neck when he woke up in the mornings (DC: Page 190)

A. FEELING PUNCHES (ON OBJECTS, NOT DIRECT)

Something invisible kept punching the hotel mattress, awakening the Smurls (TH Page 149)

VI. MISCELLANEOUS VIOLENT FELT MOVEMENT

1. VIOLENT SHAKING (OF ROOM)

A. FEELING OF EARTHQUAKE

John and Mary felt their side of the duplex shake violently from an earthquake-type of shaking (TH Loc 3639)

The chanting of the entities shook the room, rattling the windowpanes while Carolyn watched, terrified (HDHL1: Page 252)

Carolyn felt the house shaking around her (HDHL1: Page 306), (HDHL3: Page 148)

The entire house shook while Katy and Cindy screamed (HDHL2: Page 36)

Everyone in the Perron family felt the house shake multiple times (HDHL2: Page 172, 196)

An entity jumped onto Aubrey and Ellie's bed waterbed, causing it to shake and slosh violently (WDA: Page 38)

Henry felt a tremor in the ground that knocked him down (WDA: Page 141)

B. GALE FORCE WINDS (LOCALIZED)

Only on the Glatzel property, a gale force wind blew that caused trees to bend and nearly break; all other properties nearby were unaffected (DC: Page 64)

The bed was levitated in camper was jerked around mid-air (Th Loc 3007)

Kate, a neighbor of the Glatzels, experienced the gale force winds that only seemed to be targeting a certain area (DC: Page 84)

C. OTHER VIBRATION /SHAKING

The Snedeker family (and relatives) felt the house shake (IDP Loc 3178, 3184)

The family felt the house shake repeatedly from being pounded on from the inside (IDP Loc 3410)

Ed and Lorraine felt the floor vibrate (IDP Loc 4381)

Jack and Janet's mattress was shaken violently, awakening them (TH Page 148, 150, 159)

The hayloft would shake for no discernible reason when the Perron girls played up there (HDHLI: Page 211)

The entire house vibrated, which was felt by the entire Perron family (HDHLI: Page 309)

When the entity slammed the door, the entire house vibrated with the intensity of the slam (HDHLI: Page 450)

Kevin and Holly felt their floors begin to vibrate, which only grew in intensity (WDA: Page 13, 24)

The sound of the vibration that woke the Glatzels up made small objects move around (DC: Page 80)

I. FROM FURNITURE

Al felt the bed vibrating (IDP Loc 1653), felt it several more times (IDP Loc 1973, 2178, 2456)

Carmen felt the bed vibrating (IDP Loc 1887)

Both Carmen and Al felt the bed vibrating (IDP Loc 1989)

The Smurls felt their van vibrate while driving home (TH Page 120)

Maurice felt the ladder he was on shake violently from an unseen force (SH Loc 1733)

The Perron girls felt their beds shake numerous times (HDHL1: Page 206)

Cindy felt her bed shake every night (HDHL1: Page 210, 430)

Carolyn awoke to her headboard vibrating (HDHL1: Page 251)

The bed began to shake violently in front of Ed and the legs of the bed slammed on the floor (DC: Page 232)

2. RAPID, UNNATURAL ACCELERATION

The car began to accelerate on its own with the pedal being pushed down by an invisible force, felt by the driver (SH Page 139)

While the car had been in park and idling, it suddenly began to race and the pedal pushed to the floor; even when turned off, the engine kept going loudly (DC: Page 160)

The speedometer on the Glatzel's car went nuts when a funeral home by the Warrens' house was passed (DC: Page 198)

VII. OTHER TYPES OF FELT MOVEMENT (NON-VIOLENT)

1. FEELING A GRAVITATIONAL PULL /BEING DRAWN IN

When Cindy fell into the well, she felt herself pulled into it after intense vibration (HDHL2: Page 116)

Nancy felt her body being pulled towards the ground (HDHL2: Page 186)

A. VORTEX (FELT)

Jack felt a vortex of forces around him and his wife (TH Loc 1259)

Nancy felt herself pulled into the old cellar hole by a vortex (HDHL2: Page 134, 180)

Carolyn felt a vortex-like wind whip through her house (HDHL3: Page 148)

B. TILTING OF ENTIRE ROOM

Everyone felt the room tilt, feeling the loss of balance (IDP Page 337)

2. BEING TOUCHED (NON-SEXUAL)

Jerry had been touched a couple times while in the car with the entity (HDHLI: Page 466)

Arne was tapped on the shoulder twice while he was in the Newport house (DC: Page 40)

Laura felt her legs touched by small hands (IDP Loc 4512)

Jack felt a caress on his shoulders while lying in bed (TH Page 24)

Roger felt a woman caress his shoulders then back several times throughout his time in the house (HDHLI: Page 230), (HDHL2: Page 113, 123, 125, 198)

Cathi felt her long hair be touched by something when nobody was with her (HDHLI: Page 235)

A. TICKLING

Jack felt the bottoms of his feet being tickled by something he couldn't see (TH Loc 1266)

B. HAIR RAISING (WHEN TOUCHED)

When touched by the entity, Jerry's hair stood up (HDHLI: Page 466)

C. CRAWLING

Carl felt something crawling on his right leg (BN: Page 29)

D. SCALY

Debbie felt scales one night when something was touching her while she tried to sleep (DC: Page 216)

3. BEING CARRIED

Christine must have been carried to the box since she couldn't even lift the lid to get inside (HDHLI: Page 355)
Sarah felt a scraggly beard brush against her face (WDA: Page 156)

4. FEELING OF SOMEONE OR SOMETHING BRUSHING PAST

Carmen felt someone brush past her, a faint rubbing against her (IDP Page 105)
Something moved past Kevin and Holly, out of the room (WDA: Page 28)

A. WET/SLIMY FEELING ON BODY

Carmen felt something wet and slimy brush by her (IDP Loc 3831)
Tammy had the feeling of something wet and slimy slip into bed beside her (DC: Page 46)
Judy felt something wet and slimy on her arm as she made her way back to bed (DC: Page 67)

X. FEELING OF SOMETHING BEING WRONG WITH A PLACE /OF EVIL /INTENSE DISLIKE

Stephen initially felt something wrong with the place upon entering and tried to tell him mother so (IDP Page 13)

Tanya felt something was wrong with the house each time she entered it (IDP Page 142)

Laura didn't like the house after sleeping there, felt darkness (IDP Loc 2879/2895)

Diane felt something was wrong with the place when she began to walk around it (TH Loc 1043)

Ralph felt a menacing aura in the basement (BN: Page 17-18)

Judy felt that there was something wrong with the new house, stating almost immediately that she didn't like it, that it was creepy, and "not a happy home" (DC: Page 20)

When Ralph entered the laundry room during a case, he was met with horrible dread and a feeling of menace (BN: Page 87)

The tenant explained that she felt a strong presence of evil on the stairs, as did friends of hers (BN: Page 179)

Mike's young son claimed something scary lived upstairs (BN: Page 267)

Cindy felt weirded out by something in the room with her and described it as "creepy" (HDHL1: Page 209)

The house began to have a distinct feeling of dread for Bob and Lesa, making them feel uneasy about their new home (WDA: Page 94)

Cathi felt horrible dread while she was in her car (HDHL1: Page 235)

Jennifer and Megan both reported feeling afraid while in the Newport house (DC: Page 140)

When Ed stepped into the room, he immediately felt the dread of an evil presence (DC: Page 232)

I. DARK AURA OR OPPRESSIVE WEIGHT (PLACE)

Father George felt the house had a dark aura (IDP Loc 4442, 4464)

Jack had dark feelings associated with a camping trip (TH Loc 2042)

There was a very dark aura filling up the house, felt by all (HDHL2: 173, 192)

Carolyn felt a strange, oppressive weight in the air while packing the family's things up (HDHL3: Page 165)

Eventually, the house filled with a dark aura that felt heavy (WDA: Page 94)

Sarah couldn't sleep because of a feeling of ominous dread in her home (WDA: Page 156)

The clergyman sensed the dark aura of the house (WDA: Page 162)

Lori and Nancy tried to open the door, but it was too heavy for them to get open (HDHL2: Page 24, 25)

Tanya, a family friend, felt particularly claustrophobic in the Snedeker house (IDP Loc 1956)

1. TINGLING (NEGATIVE ENERGY)

Father Nolan felt a negative energy buildup from the house that made his skin tingle (IDP Page 330)

2. AVERSION TO SPECIFIC PLACES

Stephen felt a bad, dark feeling in his room (IDP Loc 567)
Carmen didn't like being in the basement (IDP Loc 1432)
Often, there was a feeling of dread associated with the property, as if something dark was underneath it (HDHL2: Page 120)
Holly particularly didn't like the parlor because the room made her feel uneasy (WDA: Page 15)

Y. TEMPERATURE FLUCTUATIONS (EXTREME)

I. BOILING / HOT PHENOMENA

The Glatzels experienced the temperature rise uncomfortably over the course of ten minutes (DC: Page 157)

1. HOT BREATH ON ONE'S BODY

John felt the reptilian beast's hot breath on his face (IDP Loc 4619)
Cindy felt this corpse-like entity's breath on her throat and at the back of her neck (HDHL1: Page 349)

2. HOT RAG ON ONE'S FACE

Some people report that they felt a hot rag on their face during sexual attacks (BN: Page 30)

II. FREEZING

1. ROOMS / SPECIFIC AREAS

The air in basement became extremely cold for Carmen (IDP Loc 1438)
The bathroom air suddenly felt cold to Laura (IDP Loc 3393)
Small sections of Snedeker house became cold multiple times (IDP Loc 3655)

Carmen and Laura felt the room get unnaturally cold (IDP Loc 3815)

Lorraine felt a freezing cold in the basement (IDP Loc 4005)

John felt the house become freezing (IDP Loc 4575)

Father Nolan felt the house was much colder than it should have been at that time of year (IDP Loc 4683)

The Smurl duplex was freezing when the temperature read 70-degrees (TH Loc 431)

Ricky felt the room freeze while investigating the Smurl duplex (TH Page 84)

Ed felt the freezing cold air of a room he went into in the Smurl duplex (TH Loc 1540, 1568)

There was a serious drop in temperature felt by Janet and Chris (TH Loc 1813)

One of the reporters felt extremely cold in the house (TH Loc 3352)

Gabby felt the room get very cold on a warm night (BN: Page 7)

DJ felt the room get cold when the apparition of his grandfather appeared (BN: Page 24)

Ruth gets cold first and would shiver uncontrollably when the entity appeared (BN: Page 27)

Brother Andrew felt two distinct area of intense cold in the house (BN: Page 78)

Often, the temperature would plummet in the Perron house as something entered the room with them (HDHL1: Page 128, 131, 134, 137, 155, 187), (HDHL2: Page 174, 191)

Cindy was visited many times by an entity that made the room ice cold upon its arrival (HDHL1: Page 206, 209, 435), (HDHL2: Page 22, 50, 253), (HDHL3: Page 169)

Nancy had several experiences where the room became freezing (HDHL1: Page 208, 212)

Cathi felt "unbearable cold" in her car (HDHL1: Page 235)

Carolyn felt the temperature become frigid as many entities entered the room (HDHL1: Page 251)

On a hot night, something stole all the heat in Jerry's car (HDHL1: Page 466)

Roger felt the temperature drop several times when he

was approached by an entity in the house (HDHL2: Page 123, 125)

Guy and Frankie felt frozen while staying in the Perron house (HDHL2: Page 246)

Kevin and Holly both felt the room suddenly become freezingly cold (WDA: Page 26)

Aubrey and Ellie's room was "as cold as a refrigerator" when Judy got there (WDA: Page 38)

Doris' bedroom was unnaturally cold, which researchers noticed upon entering the room (WDA: Page 70-71)

Liam felt intense cold in Sarah's house in the middle of summer no matter how much he turned up the thermostat (WDA: Page 160)

The clergyman who came into the house felt how cold it was (WDA: Page 162)

Though it was hot in the house, Debbie felt a horrible chill coming from in the hall underneath the attic pull-down door (DC: Page 17)

Arne felt the hair on his arms raise from cold in the summer heat while investigating the attic (DC: Page 58)

Something moved around the Glatzel home, chilling the air as it went (DC: Page 95)

A cold entity was stationed in the Glatzel's hallway, which prevented the boys from accessing their rooms (DC: Page 96)

Each time the "beast" showed up, it was extremely cold in that area (DC: Page 151, 157)

2. PEOPLE

Ruth is usually the first person to get cold when the entity enters the room (BN: Page 27)

Carolyn was constantly cold in the house, no matter what she did (HDHL1: Page 214, 510)

Barbara felt a chill go through her three times that felt like death each time (WDA: Page 37)

Ed felt a passing chill cross through the room, as if the room was being robbed of its warmth by the entity (TH Page 91)

133

John always felt cold no matter what he did (TH Loc 2673)

There was a constant cold feeling in the Perron home (HDHL1: Page 49)

Cindy felt like she was encased in a block of ice at one point (HDHL2: Page 116)

Nancy became frozen solid and couldn't move (HDHL1: Page 212), HDHL2: Page 186)

Jerry felt a freezing breath on his neck and shoulders (HDHL1: Page 466)

When Arne threw a punch at the entity, his body became numb with cold (DC: Page 157)

A. ICY TOUCH/GRIP

Chris felt an icy hand on his body (IDP Loc 4527)

Donna felt something icy touch her (BN: Page 270)

Debbie felt a very cold hand touch her at night (DC: Page 216)

III. FLUCTUATING BETWEEN HOT & COLD

The Theriault house fluctuated between hot and cold at one point (SH Loc 2631)

Z. FEELING A PRESENCE THERE (MALICIOUS)

Stephanie told Stephen she felt a presence in the room with her (IDP Loc 1042)

Laura felt someone or something was in the room with her (IDP Loc 2918)

Carmen and Laura both detected a presence in the room with them (IDP Loc 3815)

Dawn sensed a presence with her while she was in the bathroom (TH Loc 1989)

Ed felt a presence with them while talking to Janet and Jack (TH Page 216)

Carl felt something in the room with him while he tried to

sleep (BN: Page 29)

An unnamed tenant felt something was right behind her on the stairs (BN: Page 179)

Roger sensed a presence was in the room near him (HDHL1: Page 134, 450)

Freddy sensed the entity been in the van with him and Nancy (HDHL1: Page 427)

Jerry felt something in the car with him when he was near the Perron property (HDHL1: Page 466)

Katy and Cindy felt the feeling in the room shift to something evil being there with them (HDHL2: Page 35)

Keith felt a presence in the room with him while investigating the Perron house (HDHL2: Page 328)

Cindy felt a presence with her multiple times that scared her (HDHL2: Page 435), (HDHL3: Page 169)

Judy felt a pulsing evil from the entity in the room with her after being awakened (WDA: Page 33)

Katie and Lisa both sensed that an evil presence was near them in their bedroom (WDA: Page 40)

Serena felt something malicious in the room with her that watched her (WDA: Page 60)

Adam felt instinctively there was something in the coat closet as soon as he walked into the house (WDA: Page 95)

During the exorcism, everyone could feel a presence in the room with them (WDA: Page 134)

A presence could be felt guarding the boys' rooms, marked by intense cold (DC: Page 96)

Arne could sense a malicious present standing over him, staring at him while he was in bed (DC: Page 98)

Alan felt a presence nearby that scared him (DC: Page 142)

Ellie felt the malicious presence with her as she stared at the shadow standing at the end of her bed (WDA: Page 40)

Debbie felt extreme terror when she finally caught sight of this entity that had been tormenting David (DC: Page 91)

A friend of Brother Andrew felt intense hatred and evil coming off a creature she saw (BN: Page 83)

I. CHANGE IN A ROOM (FROM PRESENCE)

1. AIR SHIFT (NON-ELECTRICAL)

Carmen felt the air shift while in the basement (IDP Loc 3692)

A. FEELING OF PRESSURE ON EARDRUMS

The boys noticed a feeling of pressure on their eardrums, like when one is in deep water (WDA: Page 71)

2. ELECTRICAL CHARGE SHIFT /HAIR-RAISING

People report feeling electrical charges running through their body during sexual attacks (BN: Page 30)
Brady felt the electricity in the air make his hair stand on end (TH Loc 1620)
Roger felt his hair stand up during at least one experience with the entity (HDHL2: Page 125)

II. FEAR RESPONSES (RELATED TO PRESENCE)

Father Malone felt nervous during his time in the Smurl residence (TH Loc 884)
Diane felt afraid while walking through house (TH Loc 1043)
The figure Anne saw made her feel fearful (SH Loc 2677)
Jan felt nervous after an experience with several entities (WDA: Page 84)

1. GOOSEBUMPS RAISED
(UNRELATED TO ROOM TEMPERATURE)

Stephen felt goosebumps raise on his body while he was in the basement specifically (IDP Loc 562)
Luciana felt goosebumps after she heard an entity while it was invisible (BN: Page 28)
Tammy felt goosebumps raise on her skin anytime she was

near a certain door in the hall (DC: Page 46)

Carmen felt the hair on the back of her neck bristle when she checked the basement for Stephen and Jason (IDP Loc 1773)

Stephen felt his hair on the back of his neck stiffen combined with other horrible feelings when the entity manifested (IDP Page 45)

David's flesh rose on his arms in response to the footsteps heard overhead (DC: Page 77)

2. INVOLUNTARY SWEATING

Monique broke out in a sweat, terrified to even open her eyes as the entity manifested (BN: Page 90)

Brandon's brow broke out in a cold sweat when he saw the horde of spirits that had surrounded Jan (WDA: Page 85)

Kent's hands were sweating heavily as he attempted to capture Maurice's possession on camera (SH Page 284)

3. THROAT SWELLING /DRY

Stephen felt his throat swelling in fear as the entity called to him (IDP Page 64)

Carmen felt her throat swell in fear and was unable to speak (IDP Page 271)

While looking into a closet, Lorraine felt her heart in her throat (TH Page 64)

4. SKIN CRAWLING FEELING (NOT ACTUAL)

Jason and Stephen have Carmen check the basement and she experienced a skin-crawling feeling (IDP 1773)

Carolyn felt a deep skin-crawling feeling in the house that she tried to ignore (HDHLI: Page 151)

5. ELEVATED HEART RATE (FROM PRESENCE)

Stephen felt his heartrate quicken, hurting his chest (IDP

Page 64)

Janet felt her heart rate go up involuntarily while paralyzed (TH Page 31)

Ralph felt his heart beat uncontrollably fast (BN: Page 17)

Laura and Carmen felt their heart rates go up as they saw the entity (IDP Page 319)

Donna's heart began to pound while the spirit was present in the room (BN: Page 272)

Brandon's heart sped up when he saw the figures surrounding Jan (WDA: Page 85)

III. FEELING WATCHED /FOLLOWED / SOMETHING DIRECTLY BEHIND ONESELF

Stephen felt as if he is being watched when he was alone (IDP Loc 567) 60

Laura felt she was being watched while she was trying to sleep (IDP Loc 2879)

One unnamed witness kept feeling like he was being watched while he did renovations (BN: Page 224)

Nancy felt she was being watched by something invisible (HDHL1: Page 209)

Every member of the Perron family felt watched at some point or another by something they couldn't see (HDHL3: Page 13)

Holly often felt she was being watched in the house's parlor (WDA: Page 15)

Serena felt watched by something menacing but nobody was there (WDA: Page 59)

Bob and Lesa felt like they were being watched all the time in their house (WDA: Page 94, 99)

Laura felt she was being watched when she showered (IDP Loc 2918)

Janet felt she was being watched in the bathtub (TH Loc 1357)

Laura felt she was being followed while she was in the house (IDP Loc 2918)

The Salvatores often felt they were being followed when

they were on the stairs (BN: Page 164)

Roger felt he had been followed up the stairs by the entity and it would seemingly stop at the door (HDHL2: Page 125)

Judy felt something standing directly behind her while making dinner one night (DC: Page 85)

During the night, Arne was kept awake because he could feel something staring at him (DC: Page 98)

IV. FEELING IMMOBILIZED (CAN'T MOVE AT ALL)

Carmen felt immobilized when the entity swallowed her (IDP Loc 3692)

Janet felt she couldn't move her arm when she saw a mist (TH Loc 2734)

While in the car as Maurice lost control, Nancy couldn't move at all to help him (SH Page 140)

While in the storage room, Ralph became overwhelmed with terror to the point that he physically couldn't move (BN Page 17-18)

Carl felt paralyzed by the entity prior to a temporary possession (BN: Page 29)

Many people have reported feeling immobilized during sexual attacks (BN: Page 30)

Annie was unable to move when her mother's screams woke her up (HDHL1: Page 219)

Cindy experienced immobilization several times when nearby the entity (HDHL1: Page 222, 347), (HDHL2: Page 49)

Carolyn found she couldn't move at all during several experiences with phenomena (HDHL1: Page 306), (HDHL3: Page 148)

Cindy could not move or speak when she was pulled into the well (HDHL2: Page 116)

Guy and Frankie felt they couldn't move in the presence of an entity (HDHL2: Page 246)

Judy couldn't move during an experience with an entity in the room with her (WDA: Page 33)

Katie remembers feeling immobilized by the presence in hers and Lisa's room (WDA: Page 40)

The granddaughter reported feeling like she couldn't move while being choked simultaneously by the entity (WDA: Page 125)

Sarah couldn't move during the entity's attacks (WDA: Page 156, 157, 159)

I. PREVENTING MOVEMENT FORWARD (FORCE FIELD)

Janet felt she was unable to cross the room by a feeling of rushing water (TH Loc 1820)

Judy had to summon all her strength to run to her children, who were being attacked (WDA: Page 38)

AA. MYSTERIOUS ILLNESS /HEALTH ISSUES OR BODY PROBLEM

All the kids were frequently sick while living in an infested home (WDA: Page 126)

The kids would wake up with bloody noses, gums, and ears (WDA: Page 126)

I. MUSCLE /NERVE ISSUES

Maurice felt pain at one point in every muscle of his body (SH Page 225)

Family members also felt body pain when visiting along with researchers who experienced toothaches, etc. (SH Page 225)

Jessica felt her leg muscles hurt randomly after an encounter with a talking statue (SH Page 264)

Horrible body aches that seeped into her bones plagued Donna (BN: Page 271)

Carolyn's neck and body continually ached during her tenure in the house (HDHL1: Page 335), (HDHL2: Page 459)

Brandon randomly began to feel pain in his lower back from crushed discs but there was no injury to cause that (WDA: Page 90)

Researchers felt toothaches while investigating (SH Loc 2631)

Shoulder pain randomly started up on LaToya combined with a headache (WDA: Page 134)

Carmen experienced stiffening of body (IDP Loc 4219, 4332)

Carmen had convulsions during second illusion experience (IDP Loc 4338)

II. HEART-RELATED

Ed felt chest constriction, as if from a heart attack in the Snedeker home (IDP Page 336)

III. NAUSEA /QUEASINESS

Father George felt nausea as he approached the basement (IDP Loc 4468)

Robert felt extreme nausea during his experience (SH Page 212)

Anne felt nausea when she saw the black figure on the side of the house (SH Page 229)

Ed felt nausea growing within him when in proximity to the possessed Maurice (SH Page 284)

Lorraine felt nauseous as she walked through the Snedeker house (IDP Loc 4010)

Upon entering an infested house, Ralph felt his stomach churning, like he was going to vomit (BN: Page 17)

Ralph felt better after using holy water on himself but was very queasy after an experience with the entity (BN: Page 175)

While in the well, Cindy felt intense nausea (HDHL2: Page 116)

Aubrey suddenly felt unwell and disoriented by the presence (WDA: Page 41)

Janet heard the hybrid snorting, and the sound made her feel nauseous (TH Loc 2815)

IV. HEAD

1. MIGRAINES/HEADACHES

In proximity to the entity, Robert felt his head hurting badly and a spinning sensation (SH Page 212)

Donna felt a horrible headache every time she tried to leave the house (BN: 271, 273)

LaToya began to experience a terrible headache and had to leave the room (WDA: Page 134)

The priests involved with David's case experienced horrible headaches (DC: Page 230)

A. DIZZINESS/LIGHT-HEADED
FEELING/DRAINED/COLLAPSING

Ralph felt himself almost black out while in a demonically infested space (BN: Page 175)

Carolyn collapsed several times onto the hearth (HDHL1: Page 249, 277-278)

I. IN SPECIFIC AREAS

One corner of the room made Chris dizzy (SH Loc 3007)

Each time someone went into the cellar, it drained their energy (HDHL2: Page 118)

V. FEVER AND/OR SWEATING

Carin became very ill suddenly with a mysterious fever (TH Page 113)

Father Malone became very sweaty while talking in the Smurl house (TH Loc 884)

VI. BLURRED VISION /BLINDNESS

Laura was unable to see after a brief after an encounter with the entity (IDP Page 321)

Robert's vision whited out when he'd had an experience with the entity tormenting Maurice (SH Page 212)

VII. STOMACH ISSUES

1. PAIN

Robert also felt intense stomach pain and nausea during his experience with the entity (SH Page 212)

2. VOMITING

Robert vomited all night long after encountering the entity earlier that day (SH Page 213)

David began to vomit from stomach pains while being attacked (DC: Page 124)

David experienced vomiting after being punched in the stomach (DC: Page 146)

3. NO DESIRE TO EAT

Carolyn wasn't as hungry as she used to be and began to decline food (HDHL2: Page 460)

VIII. WEIGHT-RELATED

Carin lost a lot of weight from an unidentifiable illness (TH Page 112)

Carolyn lost so much weight that a new outfit on her made her look like she was withering away (HDHL1: Page 247)

David began to obsessively eat after the demonic activity started, which made him gain a lot of weight (DC: Page 88)

IX. LUNG /THROAT ISSUES

1. UNABLE TO BREATHE /LACK OF AIR

Carmen and Laura felt their breathing become short as an entity manifested in the room (IDP Page 318)

Carmen's breath was suddenly taken from her (IDP Page 271)

Ed had trouble breathing (IDP Page 336)

Cindy felt herself suffocating while she was trapped in a box as if there was no air (HDHL2: Page 55)

Katie also had trouble breathing in the presence of the entity (WDA: Page 40)

Cindy felt her airways being compressed while her mattress and bed were levitating and thrown around the room (HDHL3: Page 170)

A. VOCAL CORDS NOT WORKING

Shaylee sat up but couldn't scream during the interaction with an entity (WDA: Page 115)

At least one of the priests involved with David's case experienced losing their speaking voice (DC: Page 230)

2. HYPERVENTILATION

BB. FEELING AN INJURY

I. STABBING /CUTTING/SLICING/PIERCING FLESH

Al felt the sensation of being stabbed (IDP Page 242)

Laura felt her flesh being sliced open (IDP Loc 4548)

Luciana's face was cut in front of investigators (BN: Page 32)

Eleonore felt her skin being scratched as a part of a cluster of phenomena that hurt her (WDA: Page 104)

Eleonore felt she had been stabbed several times (WDA:

Page 104)

David's injuries from being stabbed, though not manifested in reality, were extremely real to him (DC: Page 105, 121)

David also felt as if he was being stabbed (DC: Page 214)

1. FEELING CLAWS

The Snedekers felt claws from smoke tendrils (IDP Loc 4774)

Luciana felt that she was clawed by something during the night (BN Page 26)

2. FEELING OF PINPRICKS

Eleonore felt her skin being pricked by an invisible entity (WDA: Page 103)

3. STINGING

Researchers felt as if they were being stung in the Snedeker house (IDP Loc 4371)

The Snedekers felt stinging on their skin throughout their near-sleepless nights (IDP Page 309)

A. BEE STINGS

Peter felt as if he had been stung by bees (IDP Loc 3326)

4. FEELING BITING

Luciana felt herself being bitten several times (BN: Page 25)

Both Brian and his older brother were bitten at different points in time (WDA: Page 69)

The Cranmer family was bitten a few times in the house (WDA: Page 95)

Eleonore felt bites from this mysterious entity tormenting her (WDA: Page 104)

IV. FEELING OF STRANGLING /SQUEEZING

David felt his face squeezed so hard by the entity that his lips were puckering outward (DC: Page 70)

V. FEELING PINCHING /POKING /PRODDING

Carmen feels pinches by an unseen force (IDP Loc 3528)

Researchers were pinched day and night in the Snedeker house (IDP Loc 4371)

Everyone in the Snedeker house began to be prodded by an invisible force (IDP Page 320)

Invisible fingers poked Laura in the eyes during Mass (IDP Loc 4706)

Laura was poked all over her body without mercy at one point (IDP Page 336)

Luciana felt her fingers being pinched (BN: Page 28)

Every time David closed his eyes to sleep, one of the entities would poke him in the eye (DC: Page 86)

VI. FEELING PUNCHES /
HITTING /BEING SLAPPED /KICKED

Jack and Janet felt punches from an invisible force (TH Loc 2386)

Luciana repeatedly experienced punches (BN: Page 25, 28)

Luciana had her head slammed against a table (BN: Page 28)

Cindy was dragged hard enough from her bed that her head hit the floor (HDHL2: Page 71)

David felt hit when he was thrown backward in full view of his family (DC: Page 68); he was also hit in the head a few moments later (DC: Page 68)

Researchers were slapped all throughout the night when they stayed at the Snedeker's home (IDP Page 309)

Janet felt a slap in her bedroom (TH Loc 75)

Luciana was slapped twice by the entity on Halloween night (BN: Page 28)

Brian and his brother had been slapped awake by something (WDA: Page 69)

David was slapped by the invisible entity in front of his family (DC: Page 68)

Jack felt he was kicked while he was driving (TH Loc 2558)

Luciana was repeatedly kicked (BN: Page 25)

Jason had bruises from a time he'd been outside playing when something invisible kicked him (DC: Page 95-96)

David was repeatedly punched, kicked, and hit by an invisible entity before undergoing possession (DC: Page 68, 92)

VII. FEELING OF BROKEN BONES /DISMEMBERMENT

Samantha felt as if her finger had been broken and indeed looked like it was as it had gone white (WDA: Page 134)

Cindy felt as if her legs were being dismembered from her body (HDHL2: 71)

VIII. BURNING

Jack felt his legs being scalded in the middle of the night (TH Page 166)

Katie complained of her stomach burning like it was on fire (WDA: Page 34)

IX. SWELLING

Megan's eye swelled after being poked (TH Loc 3379)

X. TRIPPED

Jason was tripped by the entity who grabbed his ankle while invisible (DC: Page 107-108)

Ed was tripped by an invisible entity as he tried to make his way up the steps to an infested home; the doctor with him also tripped (DC: Page 112)

XI. SHOT

David was thrown backward as if he'd been shot several times; the only thing missing was the sound of a gun and the injury, though David appeared dead for a moment (DC: Page 93, 124, 133, 214)

XII. CLUBBED

David felt himself be clubbed painfully by the entities (DC: Page 193)

CC. DISPOSITION CHANGE
(OTHER PEOPLE EXPERIENCING EFFECTS)

I. NEGATIVE PERSONALITY SHIFT

Stephen's mood became increasingly dark the longer he slept in the basement (IDP Loc 1575)

1. MOOD DISRUPTION

A. NEWFOUND ANGER ISSUES /UNUSUALLY SHORT-TEMPERED /HOSTILITY

Al's mood was increasingly angry (IDP Loc 1299), often short-tempered in general (IDP Loc 2081, 2514, 3242-3247, 3359)
Stephen became increasingly angry and rude to his mother (IDP Loc 1901, 2051)
Jack became short-tempered when once was very easy-going (TH Loc 571, 692)
Dominick began to fight more with family due to his newfound hostility (BN: Page 12)
Luciana became very hostile towards her fiancé (BN: Page 27)
Jill began to feel horrible hostility and hatred in the small

amount of time after moving in to the new place (BN: Page 77)

Timmy slapped the baby when he had never done anything violent like that before (BN: Page 77)

Roger's temper would unleash on any person nearby during and after phenomena took place (HDHL1: Page 376, 377), (HDHL2: Page 191)

Debbie exploded with anger uncharacteristically while in the infested Newport house (DC: Page 17)

David, normally happy-go-lucky, was newly rude in his answers when he wasn't being withdrawn after spending time in the Newport house (DC: Page 26)

Debbie witnessed Arne and his mother arguing heatedly while in the infested house (DC: Page 42)

Carl Jr. became hateful and angry in his dealings with his family that ended in shouting matches or violence (DC: Page 53, 76, 87, 95, 174)

Arne's mother, Mary, became heatedly angry at Arne and Debbie for backing out of the Newport house, essentially disowning them both and was continually hostile and bitter (DC: Page 83, 140)

B. DEPRESSION

All the Smurls (including their relatives on the other side of the wall) showed signs of depression while living in a demonically infested house (TH Page 221)

All the Smurls were showing signs of depression (TH Loc 3644)

Luciana radiated depression and misery after repeatedly being picked on by the entity (BN Page 20)

C. CRYING JAGS /SOBBING UNCONTROLLABLY

Mary had crying jags during her depression (TH Loc 2024)

D. SILENT PERIODS /WITHDRAWAL/DISTANT

Mary became silent and withdrawn during depression (TH Loc 2024)

Al seemed distant from Carmen, as if he were never fully present with her (IDP Page 118)

Al became quieter in general as they continued to live in the house (IDP Page 181)

Carolyn became very reclusive, uninterested in the outside world and even uninterested in her own family (HDHL1: Page 227), (HDHL2: Page 342, 445)

David also became oddly withdrawn after being in the Newport house (DC: Page 26)

E. CONSTANT NERVOUSNESS /NEWFOUND ANXIETY

Father George noted Carmen and Laura's noticeably slow and anxious speech patterns (IDP Page 315)

Luciana began to speak as if she was not young anymore (BN: Page 27)

Jack became an anxious person out of nowhere (TH Loc 3479)

Laura never felt that she could relax in the Snedeker home (IDP Loc 2912)

The Smurls felt anxiety upon returning to the house (TH Loc 3308)

II. MISCELLANEOUS SYMPTOMS /
BEHAVIORS /PHENOMENA

1. EXHAUSTION /LACK OF ENERGY

Andrea felt exhaustion after a night of sleep because an entity had manifested in the room and interacted with her while she was still asleep (her sister witnessed it) (HDHL2: Page

73)

Jack constantly felt exhausted while living in the duplex (TH Loc 1120)

Donna began to sleep much more than was normal for her (BN: Page 271)

Carolyn was consistently exhausted while living in the farmhouse (HDHL2: Page 460)

2. INSOMNIA

Jack developed insomnia though exhausted much of the time (TH Loc 1120)

Carmen and Al had trouble sleeping after awhile of living in the house (IDP Loc 1572., 1595)

3. INCREASED ALCOHOL USE

Al began to use alcohol as a method to deal with spirit activity (IDP Loc 1983, 2461, 2508, 2649, 3178, 3757, 3778)

4. DEVIANCY

A. MOLESTATION OF FAMILY MEMBERS

While under oppression, Stephen attempted to molest his cousins, Laura and Mary (IDP Loc 2956-2962, 2974)

B. IMPULSE /ACTIONS TO MAIM OR KILL OTHERS

Ellie would feel the urge to stab someone while cooking with knives in the infested home (WDA: Page 39)

Carl Jr. stabbed his brother Alan in the stomach with a metal rake (DC: Page 252)

Carl Jr. would often join in on David's attacks, laughing and cheering while his brother was hurting their family (DC: Page 187)

C. THREATENING VIOLENCE OR MURDER

Carl Jr. threatened to run over Debbie or his mother with his motorbike if he saw them in the driveway (DC: Page 76); he also threatened to shoot Debbie and often gave his mother bruises (DC: Page 252)

Carl Jr. also threatened his mother saying she should be killed and that he should be the one to do it (DC: Page 88)

Carl Jr. threatened to hurt the Warrens once he'd heard they were coming over to the house (DC: Page 161)

D. LAUGHING AT VICTIMS

Carl Jr. would always insert himself into the madness, laughing at David's attacks and cheering him on (DC: Page 187)

E. DESTRUCTION OF PERSONAL PROPERTY

Carl Jr. began to target Arne specifically: destroying his clothes, tapes, cartons of cigarettes, his new boots (DC: Page 252)

III. MISCELLANEOUS EXPERIENCED PHENOMENA

1. TARGETED PHENOMENA (SOME EXPERIENCE, SOME DON'T)

Leah experienced none of the terror of multiple sets of phenomena that her younger sisters, Megan and Jennifer experienced (DC: Page 141)

2. NEWFOUND ABILITIES (DURING INFESTATION & OPPRESSION)

A. REMOTE VIEWING

David now displayed the uncanny, accurate ability to tell what was going on in the Newport house at any given time or saw the entities traveling (DC: Page 29, 30, 50-51, 55-56, 71, 77, 98, 139, 232)

B. SEEING THROUGH WALLS

David now had the ability to see through walls, which developed over time (DC: Page 119)

C. SECOND SIGHT (ABLE TO SEE INVISIBLE ENTITIES)

David often saw the entities that began to haunt his family's home but though the family saw when the entities affected the environment, only David could see them (DC: Page 64, 67, 70, 75, 81, 86, 89, 105, 107-108, 166, 229)

Debbie was briefly able to see the entity David had described as it stared her down (DC: Page 90, 155)

At times, the entities would appear to David while he was alone and threaten him (DC: Page 99-101)

At one point, the flies that manifested in the Glatzel house were seen by David in the spirit and saw them released by the entity he called "the Beast" (DC: Page 143)

David saw the entities in the house spit in the Glatzel's food, stroke the women's thighs, shut off the heat and air conditioning, riling up the family pets, banging on the walls, and throwing holy candles; they also often spoke of hatred and of death (DC: Page 166-167)

David had been able to see the entities even after his and Arne's possessions (DC: Page 296); David also claimed to see the spirit of Alan after he died (DC: Page 296)

Arne also developed the ability to see the entities, who plagued him in prison (DC: Page 296)

A blue orb that David had seen previously was manifesting in the room, but only he could see it (DC: Page 144)

I. PROJECTING VISIONS (NON-ILLUSIONS)

The "beast" showed David a play-by-play vision of the stabbing later, who filled in his family about what was going on (DC: Page 275)

DD. ILLUSIONS (FELT)

I. ENTITY SWALLOWING ONE'S BODY WHOLE

Carmen felt an entity swallow her within itself, trapping her (IDP Loc 3692)

II. FEELING OF FALLING (NOT ACTUAL)

Judy felt herself falling when she was immobile on her bed (WDA: Page 34)

III. INJURY (NOT ACTUAL)

David felt his head wrenched all the way around until he was looking backwards (DC: Page 175)

1. SWELLING (NOT ACTUAL)

Al watched as Carmen's throat swelled up unnaturally as she slept (IDP: Page 307)

2. CUTS/SLASHES

Father Sheehan flinched when David projected a cut and found one on his leg though David didn't touch him (DC: Page 223)

THE POSSESSION CLASSIFICATION SYSTEM

Possession is what people think of when they think of demons; it's what fascinates humanity the most – that ability to control another's consciousness, body, and their actions. A major fear for the public is the idea that a demon could commit murder while in someone's body or do something similarly unforgivable and hurting someone they love. It is possible for demons to take over someone so completely that they commit murder, but it is not probable and incredibly rare. I've only found less than five instances where the person was clearly possessed at the time of the murder. It can happen, but don't go around assuming demons are behind all murders. Humans are evil, too; they're also mentally ill, which is why mental health is evaluated first long before exorcists get involved. Even with the presence of "Satanic" imagery in a case, my immediate question is, "What phenomena was present?" Violence is usually directed at the body of the possession or at the people trying to help. There

is not enough evidence linking demons and murder for the public to be afraid of it. The probability is so low that you're even dealing with a demon in the first place, and even lower that murder will be involved if one were to become possessed.

What really distinguishes demonic possessions is the lack of humanity, of humanness in behavior but jinn and other types of spirits can act like animals. The separation in my mind, then, is the appearance of impossible negative miracles along with this lack of humanity. A demon-possessed person will cause things to happen that bend how we view the world around us such as manipulating the laws of physics—in an infested house, literally anything could happen. The reason I felt the need to make an entirely new classification system for possession is that when one is dealing with encroachment, infestation, and oppression, the phenomena is happening around people or to them from an outside force. When a possession is happening, the phenomena emanates from the possessed person themselves. The same rules don't apply, and it's a separate set of phenomena.

I want to make something clear: demons are not the only spirits that can possess a person; they are simply more well-known. If you read this book and think, "Well, I've definitely been possessed but the phenomena doesn't sound familiar," then you're dealing with a different type of possessing spirit. This possibility is much more common.

The defining features of demonic possession are trances, reported every time before someone exhibits the same types of behaviors: horrible reactions to holy relics or holy people, animalistic behavior, the appearance of unnatural knowing along with unnatural strength, terrible voices emitting from the person that don't sound human, and horrific stenches following the possessed person. Much of the time, we'll see the same phenomena repeat because that demon is using the same tricks.

Demons have also been observed to attach themselves to human spirits; the Perron house had a situation like this—the perfume and loving caressing of Roger Perron could have been from the human spirit of a woman while the sudden drop into freezing temperatures, the overpowering death smell, and the sense of a malevolent presence were most likely the demon134. The phenomena which usually happened in tandem is opposing in nature; nothing demons do is loving in the slightest towards humans. It's a dead giveaway that it is a demon one is dealing with when their presence is one of unfiltered hatred and evil.

Possession in many cases involves a willingness to open oneself up to an influence not fully understood. Sometimes the door is open through one's horrible actions but most times, I've found it's because of that willingness and curiosity. Be careful what spirits you talk to or trust.

LEGEND

RDPE = Real Demonic Possessions & Exorcisms
HD: Hostage to the Devil
DCSL = The Devil Came to St. Louis
DIC = The Devil in Connecticut

I. SEEN (OBSERVABLE PHENOMENA)

A. CHANGE OF PERSONALITY (INTO ANOTHER)

Carolyn's habits and speech became similar to the entity trying to possess her that had a demon attached to it (HDHL3: Page 272)

Michael began to yell and scream, acting erratically while trying to attack Marie (RDPE: Page 35)

When David was possessed, his expression became extremely hateful and he didn't even look like himself (DC: Page 133)

B. CHANGE OF APPEARANCE

Anna's face twisted into someone (or something) else's (RDPE: Page 59)

1. EYES

A. BULGING

When the children were temporarily possessed, their eyes would bulge out (WDA: Page 125)
Anna's eyes would bulge out (RDPE: Page 59)

B. CLAMPED SHUT

Priscilla had her eyes shut during these trances she would fall into (RDPE: Page 18)

C. WHITES OF EYES SHOWN

Carmen's eyes opened wider than should've been possible (IDP Loc 4219)
Only the whites of Maurice's eyes could be seen while possessed (SH Loc 3327)
The whites of David's eyes were seen multiple times as he was taken over by the entity (DC: Page 134, 236)

D. REDDENING / GLOWING

Anna's eyes would redden and seem to glow while under possession (RDPE: Page 59)

E. HOLLOW LOOK

Carl's eyes were hollow when the assistants looked in them, as if he wasn't there anymore (HD: Page 394)

F. DILATED

David's eyes rolled back normally, and his eyes were extremely dilated afterwards (DC: Page 133)
David's eyes became completely black as his eyes had

dilated unnaturally (DC: Page 177)

2. LOOKING UNNATURALLY OLD /HAGGARD

Thomas looked unnaturally old for such a young man (HD: Page 3)

Right after the Mass, Yves looked white, haggard, his hair standing on end, and his eyes were slits (HD: Page 118)

3. SMILE

A. EVIL /MENACING

LaToya's kids displayed evil-looking smiles when possessed (WDA: Page 125)

Thomas' face was grinning in a horrible, agonized way while the building around him burned (HD: Page 4)

When Marianne was found after wandering, a terrible smile would be on her face (HD: Page 58)

The ever-present terrible smile was continually on Marianne's face during her exorcisms (HD: Page 61)

David witnessed Jonathan's face struggling with smiles and merriment, but in a disturbing way (HD: Page 142)

4. ANIMALISTIC APPEARANCE

Michael's face became animalistic when he one day turned on Marie (RDPE: Page 35)

When Bill peered at himself in the mirror, he was shocked to see a wolf-like creature staring back at him (RDPE: Page 65)

When Arne was possessed, his features took on an animalistic appearance (DC: Page 215, 255, 262, 265)

David's eyes were crazed and animalistic when Father Sheehan attempted to approach him (DC: Page 167)

C. CONTORTION OF BODY

Priscilla's body contorted in ways that were unnatural during her seizures (RDPE: Page 18, 24)

Priscilla's tongue came out farther than tongues normally do while possessed (RDPE: Page 24)

Anna's body would contort into unnatural ways and convulse (RDPE: Page 59)

David's arms and legs were restrained, so his body arched into a bow and froze (DC: Page 245)

1. BLOATING /SWELLING

Anna's body would bloat to unnatural sizes then seemingly deflate (RDPE: Page 59)

Anna would also have her tongue and lips swollen (RDPE: Page 59)

David's stomach ballooned until his middle was twice its normal size (DC: Page 136, 239)

David's head at one point was bloated to the size of a basketball with his abdomen three times larger along with his arms, legs, and fingers (DC: Page 205); this happened again during his exorcism (DC: Page 227)

David's tongue bloated so much that it led to him not being able to breathe (DC: Page 227)

A. TONGUE /EYES PROTRUDING

David's eyes and tongue began to protrude grotesquely from his face due to his extreme bloating (DC: Page 227)

2. HARDENING

The bloating caused Anna's extremities and abdomen to be as hard as a rock (RDPE: Page 59)

3. FACE MORPHING /CONTORTION OF BODY

Jonathan's mouth was open, but his tongue and teeth couldn't be seen; his face was frozen, terrified (HD: Page 167)

Michael saw a succession of many faces come through Thomas' (HD: Page 4-5)

Michael saw a face replace Thomas's, still grinning horribly while he was on fire (HD: Page 4)

Marianne's face contorted into many lines, her mouth into an S shape (HD: Page 30)

David, while possessed, underwent horrible changes into something unrecognizable (DC: Page 177, 183)

A. UNNATURAL SHAPES

Carl was tied up by invisible bindings, which was crushing his body into a smaller shape, bending him to the ground (HD: Page 328)

During exorcism, Carl's body seems to cave in on itself and diminish (HD: Page 382)

Ronnie contorted suggestively when the entity had control over his body (DCSL: Page 167)

Marianne's face contorted into several lines with her mouth forming into an S shape (HD: Page 30)

4. DISCOLORATION

Marianne had a blue discoloration to her skin and extremities at one point (HD: Page 70)

David had blue discoloration from lack of oxygen at one point after his abdomen swelled (DC: Page 136)

D. TRANCES

Before her possession, Julia would go into a trance (RDPE: Page 30)

Clarita began to fall into trances frequently before her possessions (RDPE: Page 13)

Anna would go into a trance with her eyes shut during her exorcisms (RDPE: Page 54)

Ronnie fell into a trance many, many times during his possession episodes (DCSL: Page 139, 151, 162, 171, 175, 192)

David went into a trance and began fighting his family as they tried to help him (DC: Page 227)

In the church, Arne went into a sort of trance before cursing loudly (DC: Page 230)

After the murder, Arne was found walking along the road in a definite trance (DC: Page 249)

1. NO REACTION /UNNATURAL REACTION TO STIMULI

Clarita was pricked with needles during her trances, but had no reaction (RDPE: Page 14)

Thomas was on fire but didn't move from his place, grinning terribly (HD: Page 4)

Thomas was also laughing while he was on fire (HD: Page 4)

E. PUPPETEERING OF BODY (WITNESSED)

Ronnie's body would respond to commands issuing from him that weren't his voice (DCSL: Page 212)

The entity was using David's body like a puppet while he didn't move, but something spoke through him and evilly sneered at his family through unblinking eyes (DC: Page 144)

David began to rock back and forth, his body not under his control while his legs moved on their own (DC: Page 196)

David's mouth didn't move, his eyes didn't blink, and his muscles flexing but a voice spoke through him and fought his bonds as his family dragged him to a church (DC: Page 220)

David was bobbing up and down at one point before an attack, witnessed by Debbie (DC: Page 227)

Arne's mouth was cracked open while insults came out of it during Mass, but he wasn't speaking; the entity was speaking through him (DC: Page 231)

1. AUTOMATIC WRITING

Ronnie started tracing something in the air, which turned out to be words (DCSL: Page 175)

F. NEGATIVE REACTION TO RELIGIOUS ITEMS OR PEOPLE (WITNESSED)

1. CHURCHES OR CHURCH-AFFILIATED PEOPLE

Priscilla would have intensified seizures when the priest was near (which she couldn't have known because her eyes were shut the whole time) (RDPE: Page 18)

Anna's demons would be most aggressive towards the priests and Mother Superior (RDPE: Page 60)

David had a very negative reaction to meeting clergymen and immediately began to threaten them (DC: Page 149)

Marianne reacted negatively to anything related to crosses or churches (HD: Page 56)

2. HOLY ITEMS /PLACES/RITUALS

Julia could tell the difference between regular water and holy water though they were unmarked (RDPE: Page 29)

Anna could tell when her food was prepared with holy water versus not; she had a violent reaction and produced an animalistic reaction from her (RDPE: Page 56)

Marianne reacted negatively to anything related to crosses or churches (HD: Page 56)

Ronnie ripped Father Bishop's stole to pieces (DCSL: Page 148)

When Ronnie was around a holy relic, he spat on it then on Father Bishop (DCSL: Page 151)

Ronnie reacted with rage when holy water hit him (DCSL: Page 184); he also kept spitting out the host for over two hours when he was being baptized (DCSL: Page 187)

Ronnie ripped Father Widman's prayer book away from him (DCSL: Page 222)

Ronnie threw a bottle of holy water up at the ceiling and it shattered (DCSL: Page 225)

Ronnie hurled a crucifix and the book being used for the exorcism across the room (DCSL: Page 229)

Ronnie became extremely angry when told to kiss the image of Jesus on the crucifix (DCSL: Page 230)

David went through three sets of scapulars around his neck; if they didn't wrap themselves around his neck, he would tear them off (DC: Page 190)

David acted wild from the pain of having holy salts near him or on him (DC: Page 202)

Julia would howl in pain when holy water was used on her (RDPE: Page 29)

Ronnie writhed in pain when he was sprayed with holy water (DCSL: Page 151)

At the mention of Communion or trying to place the host on his tongue, Ronnie began to howl, bark, and scream (DCSL: Page 209-212)

Ronnie complained of the burning from the religious medals around his neck (DCSL: Page 229)

David howled with pain when Judy threw holy water at her son (DC: Page 180)

David kicked over bottles of holy water while he was possessed (DC: Page 227)

3. USING RELIGIOUS ITEMS INAPPROPRIATELY (WITNESSED)

David used a statue of the Madonna as a sex object (DC: Page 203)

G. ANIMALISTIC BEHAVIOR (WITNESSED)

Bill began to chew on the fence mesh like an animal would (RDPE: Page 63)

Michael would snap at people and snarl like an animal (RDPE: Page 36)

The nurses watched Bill's behavior change him into an

animal (RDPE: Page 66)

Marianne went through periods of spitting and growling like an animal (HD: Page 58)

Marianne often behaved like a caged animal that was desperate to be free (HD: Page 69)

Ronnie would be fine one minute and the next crouched with his eyes partially closed in a corner, growling animalistically (DCSL: Page 188)

David spit, bit, and growled like an animal when a knife was taken away from him by his father (DC: Page 220)

1. DOG BEHAVIOR

Bill turned to his friend suddenly and tried to bite his leg (RDPE: Page 65)

Bill bit one of the nurses near her elbow deep enough to bleed (RDPE: Page 66)

Ronnie howled and barked like a dog while being subdued (DCSL: Page 183)

Ronnie would bite like a dog (DCSL: Page 147, 152, 155, 167, 168, 187, 193)

David, when held with his arms around his back, he became crazed and snarled like a dog, trying to bite his mother (DC: Page 179); in the same session, David began to pant with his tongue hanging out as he berated his family (DC: Page 179)

2. CAT BEHAVIOR

Holy water in Anna's food made her act purr like a large cat (RDPE: Page 56)

3. SNAKE BEHAVIOR

Ronnie behaved like a snake, his tongue flicking out and his body gliding like a snake would (DCSL: Page 230)

4. BAT BEHAVIOR

Anna hung from the wall above the doorway like a bat, with her hands and feel (RDPE: Page 54)

H. UNNATURAL ABILITIES

1. KNOWING

Priscilla knew things about everyone in the room, things she couldn't have known (RDPE: Page 25)

The voices from Julia seemed to know a lot about anyone nearby, things that weren't common knowledge (RDPE: Page 27)

Marianne displayed knowledge she could not have known of Peter's personal life (HD: Page 32)

Jonathan could read David's inner thoughts (HD: Page 141)

Ronnie sang a song he didn't know perfectly and beautifully when possessed; Ronnie also didn't sing well (DCSL: Page 155)

Ronnie seemed to understand the Latin phrases said to him, replying to them (DCSL: Page 202)

Ronnie sensed the insecurities of everyone around him and brought them to light embarrassingly (DCSL: Page 202)

David, when possessed, could tell everyone's secrets out loud and often did, to his family's embarrassment; this included things that happened before he was born and knowledge of the future (DC: Page 151)

David displayed knowledge of the priest hearing growling outside that he couldn't have known (DC: Page 165)

The demon possessing David spoke to Ed of "visiting him" and scattering the pictures and papers Ed had of the Glatzel case (DC: Page 183)

David wasn't told about Arne's cross that was gifted to him by Father Virgulak but when possessed, he knew about it (DC: Page 202)

David knew about the priest and even described him accurately though only Arne had met him (DC: Page 204); he also was able to detail strange events that happened to the priests and named their loved ones (DC: Page 223-224)

While possessed, David spoke in a language none of the family had ever heard before (DC: Page 214)

David quoted Milton's Paradise Lost at one point (DC: Page 217)

David had no prior knowledge of what oils the priests would use and correctly understood they'd been accidentally using the wrong one (DC: Page 237)

2. RANDOM ABILITIES /POWERS

Marianne blew out the candles in the room with a random gust of air (HD: Page 66)

Ronnie was projecting his voice so loudly that it could be heard throughout the rectory (DCSL: Page 185)

Ronnie somehow broke a washbasin that was on the other side of the room (DCSL: Page 185)

3. STRENGTH

Priscilla became so strong that six men had trouble keeping her down (RDPE: Page 18)

Julia had to be restrained by at least three people because she was inhumanly strong (RDPE: Page 30)

Michael was difficult to restrain; it took several people in the group to hold him back (RDPE: Page 35)

It took many men to bring Anna down from the wall, when there should've been no way she was hanging there in the first place (RDPE: Page 54)

The bloating caused Anna's weight to go up, destabilizing her iron bedframe (RDPE: Page 59)

Bill as a child pulled a fence post out of the ground with the fence still attached when his parents couldn't (RDPE: Page 63)

Bill threw people aside in the hospital who tried to stop him (RDPE: Page 66); it took a team of people to take him down, tranquilize him, and get handcuffs on him (66)

Ronnie displayed unnatural strength for his size and age (DCSL: Page 141, 148, 164, 182, 192, 205, 223)

When his father grabbed David to stop him, David immediately broke free with unnatural strength and fought him with the equal strength of a grown man (DC: Page 191)

David's strength while possessed was incredible and unbelievable how much effort it took to subdue the child (DC: Page 221); even after long periods of struggling, David's new strength was not tired and continually resisted the exorcisms (DC: Page 223, 236)

A. DEAD WEIGHTING

Ronnie dead weighted his body while possessed so it took several people to carry him to the church (DCSL: Page 183)

Arne became as heavy as a statue and Debbie couldn't shift him at all (DC: Page 264)

4. LEVITATION

Julia would levitate during her exorcisms (RDPE: Page 30)

Carl began to levitate during astral sessions (HD: Page 362)

Ronnie, according to reports, levitated across the room, flying at Father Bowdern (DCSL: Page 169, 205)

David levitated about three feet off the bed with his back to the ceiling (DC: Page 168)

David's arms were lifted while he slept then his legs, so his limbs were all in the air while he still rested; his limbs then turns clockwise and counterclockwise in the air (DC: Page 194)

A. OBJECTS

Objects nearby would fly off shelves and fly around the room because of Julia (RDPE: Page 30)

Every book in the room comes down from the bookshelves at once during Carl's exorcism; the books were also torn (HD: Page 383)

A glass pitcher was launched across the room by unseen

hands (DCSL: Page 205)

David sent several objects across the room by looking at it (DC: Page 183, 202)

Hymnbooks were found scattered on the floor of the church after David's exorcism (DC: Page 227)

I. BROKEN / RUINED

Anything of Marianne's was regularly broken (HD: Page 58)

Marianne's clothes tore open at the seams of their own accord (HD: Page 81)

Father O'Hara described seeing the exorcist's book be dissolved by Ronnie (DCSL: Page 170)

5. FURNITURE PHENOMENA

A. CHEST OF DRAWERS

A chest of drawers belonging to Marianne rocked back and forth; the handles would rattle during the exorcisms (HD: Page 63, 81)

B. DOORS

The door to Marianne's room would open and shut continually (HD: Page 58)

I. DOORS LOCKING MYSTERIOUSLY

Carl and Alan were locked in the waterbed room, yelling for help but no one could hear them (DC: Page 23)

6. MATERIALIZATION

A. BODILY FLUIDS

I. VOMIT

The vomit from Anna was often projectile and aimed at the priest (RDPE: Page 58)

Anna would vomit 10-20 times a day a disgusting fluid, but she hadn't drunk much that day (RDPE: Page 57); she also vomited solid items like tobacco and a macaroni after not eating (58)

Ronnie also projectile vomited onto people who were in the room with him (DCSL: Page 183, 199, 222)

David vomited after the entity left his body (DC: Page 215)

II. SPIT

Ronnie would spit mucus and/or blood from all the way across the room into the priests' and their assistants faces with complete accuracy (DCSL: Page 142, 148, 151, 172, 183, 184, 199, 201-202, 222, 225, 230)

David spat in Arne's face in response at one point (DC: Page 136)

David spat in his brother's face while attacking him (DC: Page 179)

David spit profusely all over Father Virgulak, Father Sheehan, Ed, and pretty much everyone helping in response to the exorcism (DC: Page 224-225, 239)

David spat on a cross from ten feet away (DC: Page 237)

When holy oils dripped down into David's mouth, he spat them back into Father Virgulak's face (DC: Page 237)

III. BLOOD

One of the priests involved with David's case woke up to his pillow being covered in blood which transferred to his face (DC: Page 229)

Blood was all over the blade that had materialized after

Alan's stabbing (DC: Page 266); Type O blood was found on the blade, but couldn't be positively identified as Alan's (DC: Page 287)

7. ABSENCE OF MATERIAL (SHOULD BE)

If Arne had murdered Alan Bono, blood should have been all over him but there was none; not only that, Arne's fingerprints weren't on the weapon either (DC: Page 287)

8. TELEPORTATION

A. OBJECTS

I. GLOWING

A knife that had been in the kennel materialized a few minutes after Alan was stabbed mysteriously that glowed (DC: Page 266)

H. STRANGE BEHAVIOR (INHUMAN OR OUT OF CHARACTER)

Christine's murder was discovered when Michael was naked in the street, covered in blood, claiming it was the Devil's blood (RDPE: Page 38)

Marianne would be found wandering around in total darkness (HD: Page 61)

Yves couldn't remove his hands from the chalice or the bread; he wept and groaned while others tried to (HD: Page 120)

Ronnie would thrash and contort, try to violently free himself from his restraints many, many times throughout his entire ordeal (DCSL: Page 139-143, 147, 149-152, 169, 172, 185, 187, 198, 218, 222, 223, 226, 230)

Ronnie grabbed the steering wheel while his uncle drove, and they drove onto the curb; Ronnie also grabbed his mom by the throat right after (DCSL: Page 182)

David got in front of his mother and threw the phone down

when she tried to call for help (DC: Page 179)

David got fidgety and with a faraway look in his eyes while in the car, he grabbed the steering wheel and pushed his foot down on the accelerator (DC: Page 213)

David began to pace strangely when he'd previously been extremely tired (DC: Page 235); soon after, he threw a paper airplane at the priest and glared at him (DC: Page 236)

David screamed at the priests to leave once he was possessed again (DC: Page 236)

Arne was possessed with rage and repeatedly punched a hole in a wooden chest (DC: Page 256)

Arne kept Debbie back from him by glaring fiercely at her and growling (DC: Page 265)

Arne fell asleep as he was being charged with murder (DC: Page 269)

1. BOWEL MOVEMENT-RELATED

Marianne urinated and excreted on the bed (HD: Page 81)

Yves became incontinent while on the altar (HD: Page 120)

Ronnie urinated all over the bed, more than a regular person could quite a few times; he also passed gas (DCSL: Page 155, 157, 165, 168, 226)

Ronnie would laugh and scream as he urinated or passed gas (DCSL: Page 165)

2. OBSCENE GESTURES OR ACTIONS

A. MASTURBATION

Ronnie pretended to masturbate in front of the priests (DCSL: Page 166, 201)

3. FAKING NORMALCY

The entity controlling Ronnie would pretend to be normal then attack again (DCSL: Page 164)

David faked normalcy to lure his mother into being alone in a room with him before he attacked her (DC: Page 181); he also exhibited this same behavior while possessed when he was being taken to a church for an exorcism (DC: Page 220, 226, 242)

I. BODILY INJURIES OR BODY ISSUES OF POSSESSED (INCLUDING SELF-INFLICTED)

Marianne constantly had bruises and cuts on her body (HD: Page 56)

Marianne would hurt herself, hitting her head against the wall and tearing her skin (HD: Page 58)

Marianne tried to tear out her own nostrils (HD: Page 69)

Welts appeared on Marianne on all of her exposed skin (HD: Page 81)

Ronnie had marks appear on him while in the trance several times (DCSL: Page 139, 191, 198, 208-210)

Ronnie also had marks appear on him while conscious (DCSL: Page 220)

Ronnie eventually began to self-inflict his scratches (DCSL: Page 200)

Ronnie experienced pain near his kidneys; his genitals also began to burn (DCSL: Page 209)

Ronnie grabbed his aunt by the neck but instead ripped the collar of her dress (DCSL: Page 193)

Ed was hit with a backhand by David while he was possessed (DC: Page 168)

Welts and redness appeared on David's body wherever the holy water landed (DC: Page 181)

Cracks developed in David's skin from how much his skin had expanded due to the entities' control over his body (DC: Page 205)

David's body was forced to undergo physical exertion like doing sit-ups for an hour by the unrelenting entities (DC: Page 214)

When Arne was going under, his body convulsed like he was having a seizure (DC: Page 215)

David was kicked by one of the invisible entities (DC: Page 227)

David was repeatedly punched, kicked, and hit by an invisible entity (DC: Page 146)

David experienced the feeling of being whipped by the entities that had infested his home (DC: Page 146)

David felt himself be punched in the stomach by an invisible force (DC: Page 146)

David was punched in the eye at one point, witnessed by his family (DC: Page 157)

David was awoken after his limbs had been levitated by kicks to the head (DC: Page 194)

David had a figure stomp on his back while his family was trying to keep him from being levitated (DC: Page 196)

The weight loss caused Anna's head to be too big for her body (RDPE: Page 59)

As the exorcisms continued, Anna's body became emaciated which caused her to need to be fed via feeding tube (RDPE: Page 59)

David was turning blue from lack of oxygen in his body as it contorted unnaturally (DC: Page 137, 227, 239); David's breathing stopped when his body contorted at one point (DC: Page 245)

David's tongue swelled up to the point of not allowing breath into his body (DC: Page 227)

1. SPECIFIC SHAPES

Some of the marks that appeared on Ronnie were numbers or words while he was possessed (DCSL: Page 191, 198)

2. INFLICTED ON EXORCISTS /THEIR ASSOCIATES

Gerald was physically attacked by something invisible, shredding his clothes (HD: Page 173)

Gerald felt a claw inside his rectum, clawing at him from the inside and another stretching his scrotum painfully (HD: Page 173)

Gerald collapsed and a new scratch appeared on his forehead; he fell into a small pool of various bodily fluids that were probably his (HD: Page 174)

Halloran was punched by Ronnie a few times during the exorcisms (DCSL: Page 141, 165)

Ronnie would often hit and/or kick the priests whenever he could (DCSL: Page 142, 167, 172, 184, 187, 209, 223, 226)

When Ronnie's hands were removed from Father O'Flaherty, there were red welts left behind (DCSL: Page 188)

David tried to attack the priests when brought into the church (DC: Page 222); everyone, especially the priests were kicked, bitten, and punched (DC: Page 226)

When the entity faked normalcy, Father Virgulak reached down to speak to David; this led to the entity grabbing his stole and trying to choke him with it (DC: Page 226-227)

3. INFLICTED ON FAMILY / LOVED ONES

Alan fell to the ground, stabbed by the entity though no one saw him being stabbed nor was a knife seen (DC: Page 265)

Alan had five stab wounds; three of them appeared later on his body (DC: Page 267)

Arne was stabbed on the anniversary of Alan's death by the entity (DC: Page 296)

Debbie was hit in the jaw with a book during one of David's episodes (DC: Page 227)

Debbie was kicked hard in the stomach, head, and chest (DC: Page 262)

avid grabbed Arne around the neck and tried to strangle him (DC: Page 136)

David grabbed his mother around the neck and began choking her, attempting to kill her until Alan intervened (DC: Page 179); after Alan stopped him, David turned his fists and spat in his brother's face (DC: Page 179)

David grabbed his mother by her breasts then began to strangle her again (DC: Page 181); Alan intervened again and once again, was punched, flying backward (DC: Page 181)

David almost always attacked someone while under the

entity's control (DC: Page 187, 214, 227); while fully possessed, he held his visiting grandmother at knifepoint (DC: Page 220)

J. MISCELLANEOUS WITNESSED PHENOMENA

1. VIBRATION /SHAKING /TREMBLING (OF POSSESSED)

David began to shake uncontrollably all over his body during his possessions (DC: Page 133, 236, 239)
Arne would shake violently before his possessions (DC: Page 255)

2. TARGETED PHENOMENA (SOME EXPERIENCE, SOME DON'T)

Leah strangely never experienced any phenomena while in the Newport home while her sisters, Jennifer and Megan, experienced an onslaught of multiple types of phenomena through many of their senses (DC: Page 141)

3. DEMATERIALIZATION OF OBJECT

A knife appeared in David's pocket that then disappeared when Ed reached for it (by all accounts, it was physically there instead of an illusion) (DC: Page 226)

II. HEARD PHENOMENA (OR SHOULD BE HEARD)

K. DIFFICULTY BREATHING (HEARD)

Carl sounded like he was having trouble breathing properly, like he was pushing past an obstacle blocking his breath (HD: Page 328)

L. MOANING /GROANING /GAGGING / TORTURED SIGHS EMITTING FROM POSSESSED

David let out a strange moan as the spirit began to possess

him (DC: Page 133)

When David was going under, he would emit horrible, tortured groaning and moaning (DC: Page 176); he also did this while coming out of possession (DC: Page 224)

A disgusting gagging sound came from David's body right before he gained control of himself again (DC: Page 184)

David began gagging about ten minutes into High Mass (DC: Page 209)

A kind of tortured sighing came from David when the spirit was close to departing (DC: Page 247)

M. NEW VOICE EMITTING FROM POSSESSED

David started speaking aloud in a voice that wasn't his own (RDPE: Page 46)

Voices would emit from Anna, but her lips were shut the whole time (RDPE: Page 54)

Thomas spoke with a voice that wasn't his in front of his friend (HD: Page 4)

Marianne would often speak in a voice was not her own (HD: Page 30)

Marianne spoke like a puppet, as a vessel for something else to speak and as if something were whispering to her while she repeated it (HD: Page 57)

A voice came from Marianne that was neither gender, mocking and throaty (HD: Page 62)

David spoke in an evil voice while possessed (DC: Page 133, 183)

1. GUTTURAL/DEEP

The kids' voices would deepen while possessed into a voice unlike their own (WDA: Page 125)

Ronnie's body would respond to commands issuing from him that weren't his voice (DCSL: Page 200)

Priscilla's voice became very deep, guttural, and aggressive during one of her episodes (RDPE: Page 24)

Ronnie screamed in a guttural voice, protesting the

upcoming baptism (DCSL: Page 181)

Ronnie spoke in a new voice he'd never used before that was deep and dark (DCSL: Page 199); later, it came out more often and claimed to be the devil (DCSL: Page 210, 212-213, 218-219, 222, 224, 226)

David's voice became deep and hoarse, claiming he was gone (DC: Page 178); this husky man voice would often come out, spewing accusations (DC: Page 220)

Horrible voices would issue from David while the boy slept (DC: Page 204)

2. HIGH-PITCHED /SQUEAL

Ronnie often talked with a high-pitched voice coming through him (DCSL: Page 151)

A woman's voice came through David and he told his mother that the holy water burned (DC: Page 181)

3. MULTIPLE VOICES (RANGING IN PITCH)

The voices emitting from Julia ranged from deep and guttural to high-pitched (RDPE: Page 27)

Voices would emit from Anna, but her lips were shut the whole time; these voice would vary as deep or high-pitched, rageful, hopeless/grieving (RDPE: Page 54, 57)

The demonic voice emanated in the room but not from anywhere in particular, which then eventually turned into many overlapping voices together (HD: Page 73)

Two voices, one high and one similar to an animal came out of Arne during his final possession, witnessed by Debbie and Leah (DC: Page 265)

Ronnie's voice would range from guttural to high-pitched, possibly because there was more than one demon present (DCSL: Page 157)

4. MALICIOUS OR REPETITIVE LAUGHTER

Priscilla would laugh maliciously when she was able to

hurt someone (RDPE: Page 23)

Ronnie laughed in this other voice in the car repetitively; he was also laughing while they carried him to the church (DCSL: Page 181)

Ronnie laughed maliciously after hitting one of the priests in the face (DCSL: Page 209)

Ronnie would also laugh after insulting the exorcist and his assistants (DCSL: Page 212, 219)

David laughed at the family in distress as they watched him say and do horrible things (DC: Page 136)

Laughter issued from David's bedroom when his mother bade him to answer her (DC: Page 176)

David laughed evilly after the car he'd taken control of almost hit a group of people at an intersection (DC: Page 213)

When Ed reached for the knife that had been there a second ago, he found nothing and the entity laughed at him (DC: Page 226)

David laughed at the priests when they'd made a mistake with which oil to use for the exorcism (DC: Page 237)

David laughed at Arne when he said for the demons to possess him instead (DC: Page 243)

5. USING INSULTING LANGUAGE

The language the voices used through Julia was terrible and hateful (RDPE: Page 27, 30, 31)

Marianne was using inflammatory and disrespectful language many times (HD: Page 30, 58, 64)

Ronnie would curse at and insult the men trying to perform and help with his exorcism (DCSL: Page 156-158, 166-168, 181, 189, 199, 201)

Ronnie also cursed the entire way he was carried to the church (DCSL: Page 183) and then much more when he was sprayed with holy water (184)

The entity often would talk to David and say horrible things to him for the boy to repeat to his family (DC: Page 71)

David, while possessed, said horrible things to his family and anyone who tried to help, including the priests (DC: Page

134, 179-181, 220, 223-224, 237-238, 243)

David's replies right before possession became brusque and even outright rude (DC: Page 236)

A. BLASPHEMY, MOCKING RELIGION OR RELIGIOUS PEOPLE /ITEMS

The voice emitting from Priscilla began to mock others for attending church and mocking the pastor in general (RDPE: Page 24)

The voice from Julia mocked nuns and anything sacred (RDPE: Page 30)

Thomas was continually berating the priest who came to help him (HD: Page 4)

Jonathan made several comments about Jesus, God, the Church that were hateful or mocking (HD: Page 143)

Carl mocked the priests many times during his exorcisms (HD: Page 385, 386)

Ronnie would use taunts about the Virgin Mary and say prayers in an insulting way (DCSL: Page 158)

Ronnie would mock the men of the cloth with talk of sex and masturbation while possessed (DCSL: Page 169, 172, 201, 212, 218)

David would insult the use of holy water while possessed (DC: Page 133)

David insulted God, Jesus, Mary and Christianity several times during his possessions (DC: Page 136, 184, 187, 214, 222, 237)

David mocked the priest when he came into the house (DC: Page 164); he also exhibited this behavior while in the church with the priest (DC: Page 223-224)

Arne, when he was under the entity's control during Mass, began to curse and insult the church loudly (DC: Page 230)

B. THREATS

Ronnie threatened the priests' lives and safety (DCSL: Page 149, 226)

Ronnie threatened his cousin's life (DCSL: Page 194)

David threatened everyone in the room while the entity possessed him (DC: Page 133-134, 144)

When David met the clergymen, he began to threaten them both immediately (DC: Page 149)

David threatened his mother, telling her she deserved to die right before he attacked her (DC: Page 179)

David threatened Ed several times (DC: Page 183, 220)

A voice spoke through David while he slept, threatening Arne's life (DC: Page 212)

The entity inside David named the priests' loved ones and threatened them as payback for the exorcism (DC: Page 224); he also threatened anyone close to him that was helping with the exorcism (DC: Page 226, 246) and David while he wasn't there (DC: Page 242, 246)

Arne was often threatened with possession and even right before he would become possessed, the entity would say it was going to do it to him; the entity also threatened to ruin Arne's life (DC: Page 230-231)

C. SINGING RACIST /BLASPHEMOUS RELIGIOUS SONGS

Ronnie would sing racist songs several times during the ordeal (DCSL: Page 144, 167)

Ronnie sang religious songs mockingly or inserted dirty lyrics, etc. (DCSL: Page 199-201, 226)

D. SEXUAL IN NATURE

Many of the remarks Marianne made were sexual (HD: Page 30, 58, 64)

David said horrible things to his mother while possessed that were often sexual in nature (DC: Page 179, 187); David also said such things to Debbie (DC: Page 187) and to whoever happened to be nearby (DC: Page 203, 220)

6. SPEAKING IN THIRD PERSON (THROUGH THE PERSON)

Julia would talk about herself in the third person when the

other voice came out (RDPE: Page 30)

A. PUPPETEERING (HEARD)

Marianne spoke like a puppet as a vessel for something else to speak and as if something were whispering to her while she repeated it (HD: Page 57)

Carl seems to cease to be alive in body, though a voice issues from him that isn't his own that doesn't sound human (HD: Page 382, 384)

A new voice issued through David though his mouth didn't move (DC: Page 144, 168)

While David lay facedown on his bed, several noises came from his prone body: hissing, growling, and snarling (DC: Page 168)

7. EXHIBITING STRANGE LANGUAGE FLUENCY (HEARD)

Julia exhibited fluency in languages she didn't know like Spanish, Latin, Greek (RDPE: Page 27)

Michael yelled at Marie in multiple languages, switching back and forth between them (RDPE: Page 35)

David eventually began to speak in Latin (RDPE: Page 46)

Anna would understand/reply in languages she'd never heard, like Latin and German (RDPE: Page 57)

David appeared to be speaking English backwards at one point (DC: Page 195)

8. SCREAMING /SHOUTING CONTINUALLY

At one point, Marianne screamed so loud that it vibrated her whole body then wailed (HD: Page 64)

Ronnie would scream/howl as he struggled against the exorcist's assistants holding him down (DCSL: Page 164, 167, 168)

David was screaming and yelling throughout his exorcisms (DC: Page 221-225, 238)

A. SPECIFIC NAME /NAMES

Marianne, at one point, screamed Peter's name over and over (HD: Page 60)

9. MIMICRY OF OBJECTS

A. BELL SOUND

Ronnie made sounds like a bell ringing (DCSL: Page 219)

10. SPEAKING TOO
QUICKLY (UNINTELLIGIBLE) /INCOHERENT

At one point, David was talking so fast that he couldn't be understood (DC: Page 190)

Priscilla could not speak during certain times; her tongue would be stuck to the roof of her mouth and was unable to be removed (RDPE: Page 22); unfortunately, Priscilla never spoke again after this event (RDPE: Page 25)

Arne was babbling and incoherent as he was being charged with Alan's murder (DC: Page 269)

N. WHISPERINGS

Vague whisperings were coming from David's bedroom when he was possessed (DC: Page 176)

O. ANIMAL SOUNDS

1. ROARING /GROWLING /HOWLING /SNARLING / HISSING EMITTING FROM THE POSSESSED

Julia would roar like an animal during her exorcisms (RDPE: Page 31)

A growl came out of Bill, still a child at the time from the entity (RDPE: Page 63)

Bill got on all fours, growling, snarling, and snapping at people (RDPE: Page 66)

Jonathan spoke with a terrible raspy hissing quality to his voice (HD: Page 142)

Jonathan howled longer than any human would've been able to along with sobbing (HD: Page 169)

Carl began to moan, growl, and eventually seemingly yelling through his teeth (HD: Page 328)

Ronnie would make animal sounds and scream (DCSL: Page 144, 149, 218, 228)

Ronnie was behaving like a dog in the way he was snapping at Edwin and Leonard (DCSL: Page 147)

The vibration sound the Glatzels heard eventually transitioned into a low roar (DC: Page 80)

David let out an angry animal growling while threatening his family (DC: Page 134, 136); he also snarled during the same episode (DC: Page 136)

A snarling sound came out when the priest tried to get closer to David (DC: Page 164); growling also rang out in the same situation (DC: Page 167)

A snarl like a dog's emitted from David several times during his possessions (DC: Page 176, 179)

An animalistic groan came from David's bedroom (DC: Page 179)

Arne growled as if he were an animal while he was under (DC: Page 215, 262)

David was snorting and snarling when he was caught and restrained for exorcism (DC: Page 222)

Debbie was kept back from approaching Arne by a vicious snarling; he roared victoriously right after (DC: Page 265)

A. SOUND OF ANIMAL TORTURE OR DYING ANIMAL

Marianne howled from her slit-like mouth, going on for about a minute and it physically threw others back, the force of it; it was described as a wolf or a tiger being tortured (HD: Page 60)

Marianne roared, sounding like a stuck pig (HD: Page 79)

David emitted tortured animal wailing during his exorcism (DC: Page 227); he also did this when holy water was administered (DC: Page 245)

2. PACK OF ANIMALS

During Anna's exorcisms, a sound like a group of animals was heard that sounded faraway; these animals ranged from dogs barking to cats, cattle, and hyenas (RDPE: Page 57)

Animal sounds were heard throughout Marianne's exorcism; a horse, a dog, a mewing man punctuated with pain (HD: Page 70)

Priscilla would bark like a dog and bleat like a sheep (RDPE: Page 18)

P. TAILORED PAIN SOUND
(BESPOKE TO OTHERS IN ROOM)

Carl emitted a sound that tailors itself to each person's pain in the room; everyone experienced something different specific to them, which the tape didn't pick up (HD: Page 384)

Q. OVERREACTION TO HEARD STIMULI

When Marianne heard a radio, she put her hands on her ears, screaming, spun around then fell on her face while twitching (HD: Page 41)

R. FURNITURE PHENOMENA (HEARD)

Multiple thumps and furniture movement was heard in the convent once the entities had been expelled from David (DC: Page 233)

1. DOOR

The door to Marianne's room banged loudly open and shut continually (HD: Page 58)

2. CHEST OF DRAWERS

A chest of drawers belonging to Marianne rocked back and forth; the handles would rattle during the exorcisms (HD: Page 63, 81)

T. ELECTRICAL ISSUES (HEARD)

The car radio, which had been working a second ago, began to play only static while Ronnie went into a trance even while the car was off (DCSL: Page 181-182

U. MISCELLANEOUS HEARD PHENOMENA

1. PAGES RUSTLING

The Glatzels and the priests heard the rustling of the hymnbooks in the church (DC: Page 224)

2. FOOTSTEPS

Footsteps were heard walking in the church during David's exorcism (DC: Page 224)

3. GASPING/HEAVING

During his exorcism, David let out a heaving gasp as the entity left him (DC: Page 245)

III. SMELL PHENOMENA

V. UNSPECIFIED DISGUSTING SMELLS

Bill remembers smelling a terrible stench that filled his nostrils and sinuses (RDPE: Page 62)
There were terrible odors that filled the room during Ronnie's exorcisms, which continued long after Ronnie left (DCSL: Page 225)

W. TERRIBLE ODORS (SPECIFIED)

1. URINE/EXCRETA/BOWELS

Marianne urinated and excreted on the bed, which gave off a terrible smell (HD: Page 81)

David smelled dung from cow stalls and human smell of toilets (HD: Page 161)

Ronnie passed gas and urinated then the room smelled so bad that windows had to be opened and it made Father Halloran's eyes water (DCSL: Page 157, 165)

The urine Ronnie produced had a terrible smell to it, worse than the smell usually is (DCSL: Page 155, 168)

2. UNWASHED BODY/HAIR

Anyone who passed by Marianne got a whiff of unwashed hair/body though she looked clean (HD: Page 40)

A rotting smell emanated from Marianne's room, one of filth and putrefaction; it could not be covered up even by ammonia-drenched plugs in noses (HD: Page 59)

3. VOMIT

Judy was met with the smell of vomit when she walked into David's bedroom (DC: Page 176)

IV. FELT PHENOMENA (BY POSSESSED)

X. MEMORY ISSUES/LOSS

Julia had memory lapses during her possession (RDPE: Page 30)

Anna had no memory of her time being possessed (RDPE: Page 54)

Yves experienced memory gaps during his exorcisms (HD:

Page 108)

Ronnie usually couldn't remember anything that happened after he went into the trances (DCSL: Page 158)

Arne couldn't remember anything past a certain point of being possessed and didn't realize Alan was dead until he was charged with his murder (DC: Page 269)

Y. MEDICAL/BODY ISSUES/PAIN

Ronnie complained of feeling sick right before a possession episode (DCSL: Page 181)

Ronnie urinated on the bed, this time complaining how painful it was (DCSL: Page 209)

1. SEIZURES/TREMORS

Clarita began to have seizures suddenly and frequently (RDPE: Page 13)

Priscilla started to have horrible seizures (RDPE: Page 18)

Michael had convulsions that became outwardly violent (RDPE: Page 36)

Marianne had seizure-like episodes along with periods of coma along with incontinence (HD: Page 58)

Yves had his first seizure at Mass (HD: Page 116)

Jonathan's body visibly shook from a violent tremor (HD: Page 168)

Carl began to have seizures after the morning at Aquileia (HD: Page 329, 384)

A. PROLONGED (UNNATURAL)

Priscilla's seizures started to go on for hours (RDPE: Page 23)

2. HEART ISSUES

Bill felt chest pains as if he were suffering a heart attack several times (RDPE: Page 66)

Michael felt his heart begin to have problems, like a weight was on it (HD: Page 5)

Marianne's pulse became very faint at one point while possessed, observed by those with her (HD: Page 70)

3. FEVER / CHILLS / SHAKING

When the control of her body left her, LaToya recalled shaking feverishly (WDA: Page 125)

Ronnie felt sick before an episode with his feet hot then cold (DCSL: Page 175)

Z. CHANGES IN PERSONALITY (EXPERIENCED)

1. MURDEROUS URGES

A. SUICIDAL IMPULSES

Ronnie tried to jump over the bluff into the river during the day (DCSL: Page 217)

2. MOOD CHANGES

A. UNCHARACTERISTIC ANGER

David felt himself infected by the evil spirit with him, causing him to snap on another person in the room (HD: Page 144)

Priscilla began to feel murderous urges starting with her parents and even children (RDPE: Page 19)

AA. ILLUSIONS / HORRIBLE VISIONS

Anna would see visions of dark versus light battles as she would rest from exorcisms (RDPE: Page 59)

David had ugly, strange visions happen to him as something tried to take him over (HD: Page 157, 161)

Aubrey also kept imagining her hands turning into claws and hurting people with them (WDA: Page 39)

Ronnie dreamed about a huge red devil that was trying to keep him from escaping a burning pit (DCSL: Page 140)

Ronnie saw the terrible vision of a black stain; inside it was a horrible figure in a black hood (DCSL: Page 153)

Jason, Debbie's young son, saw a horrible vision of the entity spewing fire and sitting on a throne of bats (DC: Page 297)

1. ILLUSIONS OF INJURY

When the entity was asked who it was, a red blotch appeared on David's leg that then morphed into the face of a devil; this faded after ten minutes (DC: Page 195)

David projected a slash on Father Sheehan's leg and when he lifted his pant leg, he found a cut (DC: Page 223)

BB. LIGHTHEADED /WARM SENSATION

When the possession started, LaToya felt both lightheaded and warm (WDA: Page 125)

CC. FEELING SOMETHING TAKING OVER ONE'S BODY

Aubrey felt she was losing control of her hands to something else (WDA: Page 39)

Bill lost control of his mind, body, and emotions as a rage swelled within him (RDPE: Page 63, 65)

Debbie felt this entity beginning to take over her body, drawing her towards it (DC: Page 91)

1. PRESSURE IN CENTER OF BODY

When Jaymie was being taken over, he felt his mind blocked by pain and pressure building in his chest towards his center; he had a feeling of his brain being yanked on through the spine (HD: Page 253)

2. POOLING OF SENSES (REMEMBERED)

David felt his senses pool together as he was being possessed, becoming agonizingly painful (HD: Page 156)

3. FEELING OF ICY COLD (REMEMBERED)

Bill was playing in the garden when he felt icy cold sweep over his body (RDPE: Page 62); he felt this numerous times as the entity took over his body (63)

DD. UNABLE TO MOVE /IMMOBILE (REMEMBERED)

David was transfixed, unable to move to start the exorcism (HD: Page 168)

Hearty cannot move to warn the others about faking behavior during a part of the exorcism experience (HD: Page 389)

FELT PHENOMENA (NON-POSSESSED)

EE. EXTREME TEMPERATURE FLUCTUATIONS

1. FREEZING

A. ROOM

When Julia walked into the room, the temperature would drop dramatically (RDPE: Page 30)

The temperature in the room was cold on a hot day outside (HD: Page 144)

There was a chilling quality to the room that was unnatural during Ronnie's exorcisms that continued long after he was gone (DCSL: Page 224-225)

B. PERSON

Marianne was very cold physically to the touch (HD: Page

61)

Norman felt coldness enter Carl, which made him have to physically let go of Carl (HD: Page 328)

Carl's body goes cold, as if he's near death (HD: Page 391)

2. HOT

When the voices spoke through Julia, the temperature would rise unbearably (RDPE: Page 31)

FF. MURDER

1. PEOPLE

Michael strangled Christine and had also taken out her eyeballs, ripped her tongue out, tore much of the flesh on her face; all of this DNA was present under his fingernails (RDPE: Page 37)

Thomas had murdered several women and kept the bodies, which were mutilated (HD: Page 4)

2. ANIMALS

Michael had also found his mother-in-law's dog strangled and torn apart as well (RDPE: Page 38)

Kate, a neighbor of the Glatzels, had her dog brutally attacked, breaking its back, which would likely result in its death (DC: Page 196)

CONCLUSION

The paranormal is an ever-changing field as we discover new ways to study it. It is impossible at this point, and at any point, to have a true conclusion. I am using classification techniques I learned in my folklore studies to map out behavioral patterns based on the way that the experiences are reported. People's memories are malleable; nothing is 100% accurate, but some memories stay with us because of the terror we felt, even if we don't report it quite as accurately as it happened. I find value in that reporting because in the paranormal, experience is everything. It's how we understand the supernatural, through our own senses/experiences and the ones we're willing to believe other people had. Every new form of research has its flaws and at the time of this publication, I have not discovered them yet. I'll do my best to adapt and overcome any flaws in future publications while I evolve as a researcher, but for now, this is what I have. I hope it was valuable to whoever reads this and that it can be used by paranormal investigators and the public alike to identify demonic phenomena in a more cohesive

way.

Once again, demons are not as common as one might think so reexamine your biases as you attempt to identify spirit types. Exorcisms are dangerous and if you misidentify what is happening when it is mental illness or another type of spirit, not only will the exorcism fail but that person could die. It has unfortunately happened before. Proceed with caution. Also be aware that grifting happens in the paranormal. Be wary and don't fall for anyone trying to charge lots of money. Beyond that, I am not involved in getting rid of them. Hopefully, this book helps to give knowledge about this popular, often sensationalized subject.

REFERENCES

Brittle, Gerald. 2013. *The Demonologist: The Extraordinary Career of Ed & Lorraine Warren.* Reprint.

Bhayro, Siam, and Catherine Rider. 2017. "Demons and Illness from Antiquity to the Early Modern Period."

"Demon." n.d. Online Etymology Dictionary. https://www.etymonline.com/word/demon#etymonline_v_5575.

"Devil." n.d. Online Etymology Dictionary. https://www.etymonline.com/word/devil.

El-Zein, Amira. 2017. *Islam, Arabs, and the Intelligent World of the Jinn.*

Finlay, Anthony. 1999. *Demons! The Devil, Possession, and Exorcism.*

Flesher, Paul V.M. 2016. "The Three Monotheistic Religions: Children of One Father." UW Religion Today. https://www.uwyo.edu/uw/news/2016/09/uw-religion-today-the-three-monotheistic-religions-children-of-one-father.

Guiley, Rosemary Ellen. 2009. *The Encyclopedia of Demons and Demonology.*

Harker, John. 2021. *When Demons Attack: True Tales of Diabolic Encounters.*

Hufford, David. 1982. *The Terror that Comes in the Night.*

Jaye, Victoria, "In the Presence of Evil: Demonic Perception Narratives" (2021). *All Graduate Plan B and other Reports,*

Spring 1920 to Spring 2023. 1563.
https://digitalcommons.usu.edu/gradreports/1563.

Jones, Marie D., and Larry Flaxman. 2017. *Demons, the Devil, and Fallen Angels*.

Kadmon, Baal. 2019. *Devils, Demons, and Ghosts in the Hebrew Tradition: Romancing the Sitra Achra*.

Knowles, Zachery. 2017. *True Ghost Stories: Real Demonic Possessions & Exorcisms*.

Martin, Dale Basil. 2010. "When did Angels Become Demons?" Journal of Biblical Literature.

Martin, Malachi. 1992. *Hostage to the Devil: The Possession and Exorcism of Five Contemporary Americans*.

Perron, Andrea. 2011. *House of Darkness, House of Light – The True Story, Vol 1*.

Perron, Andrea. 2013. *House of Darkness, House of Light – The True Story, Vol 2*.

Perron, Andrea. 2014. *House of Darkness, House of Light – The True Story, Vol 3*.

Peterson, Mark Allen. 2007. "From Jinn to Genies: Intertextuality, Media, and the Making of Global Folklore."

Reed, Annette Yoshiko Reed. 2020. Demons, Angels, and Writing in Ancient Judaism.

Sarchie, Ralph. 2001. *Beware the Night: A New York City Cop Investigates the Supernatural*.

Taylor, Troy. 2021. *Devil Came to St. Louis: The Uncensored True Story of the 1949 Exorcism*.

Vandestra, Muhammad. 2021. *The World of Angels (Malaikah) and Demon (Jinn) in Islam Religion*.

Walton, John H. and J. Harvey Walton. 2019. *Demons and Spirits in Biblical Theology: Reading the Biblical Text in its Cultural and Literary Context.*

Wan, James, dir. 2013. *The Conjuring.*

Warren, Ed, Lorraine Warren, Michael Lasalandra, Mark Merenda, and Maurice Theriault. 2014. *Satan's Harvest.* Reprint, Graymalkin Media.

Warren, Ed, Lorraine Warren, Ray Garton, Carmen Reed, and Al Snedeker. 2014. *In a Dark Place.* Reprint, Graymalkin Media

Warren, Ed, Lorraine Warren, Robert Curran, Joe Smurl, Janet Smurl. 2014. *The Haunted.* Reprint, Graymalkin Media.

ACKNOWLEDGEMENTS

A special thanks to my mom, dad, sister, and boyfriend who continue to support my work in every way they can. My family and friends have helped more than they know to encourage me in writing this book because something really didn't want it written.